SOME FOLK SAY

SOME FOLK SAY

Stories of Life, Death, and Beyond

Jane Hughes Gignoux

illustrated by Stéphan Daigle

FOULKETALE PUBLISHING

Published by
FoulkeTale Publishing
201 West 89th Street, Suite 7H, New York, NY 10024-1848.
Tel / Fax (212) 580-1007

Every effort has been made to secure permission to use these stories. In some cases, author
contact proved impossible. I appreciate all those who assisted in the search.

"All Souls' Day" by D.H. Lawrence, from *The Complete Poems of D.H. Lawrence*
by D.H. Lawrence, edited by V. de Sola Pinto & F.W. Roberts. ©1964, 1971
by Angelo Ravagli and C.M. Weekley, Executors of the Estate of Frieda Lawrence Ravagli.
Used by permission of Viking Penguin, a division of Penguin Putnam Inc.

Publisher's Cataloging-in-Publications
Provided by Quality Books, Inc.

Gignoux, Jane Hughes.
Some folk say: stories of life, death, and beyond / Jane Hughes Gignoux;
illustrated by Stephan Daigle. —1st ed.
p. cm. Includes bibliographical references.
Summary: Retells, in prose and poetry, the legends by which diverse cultures
have come to terms with the reality of death and their hopes for life beyond the grave.
LCCN: 98-73955
ISBN 1-9667168-0-9
1. Death—Folklore—Juvenile literature. 2. Future life—Folklore—Juvenile literature. 3. Death—
Folklore. 4. Future life—Folklore. I. Daigle, Stéphan Daigle. II. Title.
GR455.G54   1998   398.27
QBI98-1521

Book design by Julia Hill Gignoux, Freedom Hill Design
Illustrations by Stéphan Daigle

Printed in Mexico

November 1998
2   3   4   5   6   7   8   9   10

CONTENTS

LESSONS FOR LIFE

AFTER DEATH

RECONCILIATION WITH DEATH

For my wonderfully wise children, who all enjoy stories
Henri, Peggy, Louise, and Paul

PREFACE

Since the 1980s the increasing AIDS epidemic has forced new segments of society to deal with death; every day young adults and children die from the effects of the virus. Untold anger, fear, resentment, and sadness surround this growing population of the infected. Yet caregivers and health professionals often have little to offer beyond personal compassion.

The genesis for this book arose out of that exact dilemma. One day several years ago, I was talking on the telephone to my friend Michael Lipson, senior psychologist for the Family Care Program at Harlem Hospital where I work with the HIV children as a volunteer. He mentioned that he was on his way to the Intensive Care Unit to visit a teenage patient. He wanted to take something to read to the boy but was hard pressed to find appropriate material. "Some day I'm going to write a book," he said. "It's going to be called *Some Folk Say,* and it's going to be a collection of stories from different cultures around the world about what happens when you die." The minute I heard that statement, something deep inside me exploded, and much to the surprise of both of us, I burst out with, "Oh, Michael, I want to help you with that project!" Up until that moment, I had no idea that I might be interested in working on such a book. Such are the surprises of life's journey.

Michael and I worked together developing the book for about a year and a half. Then it became apparent that Michael's other professional commitments were expanding to such a degree that he could no longer devote adequate attention to this project, so he agreed to withdraw. Much of his invaluable contribution remains, however, in the form of sensitive and telling commentary on some of the stories. In addition, the philosophy and purpose underlying the book were crafted out of our numerous conversations over countless cups of tea. I treasure that experience. I have missed his involvement since then, and I am deeply grateful for his ongoing friendship and support.

ACKNOWLEDGMENTS

How does one start and where does one go to find stories about death and the afterlife? I started with a call to Flo Stone in Washington, whose generous enthusiasm for this project led me to Richard Lewis, Fred Meyers, and Alan Wardwell. They graciously steered me to rich material and sent me off to libraries where a world of myth opened before me. It is my experience that most librarians are sitting behind their desks just *waiting* for me to come along with convoluted questions about obscure volumes long out of print. The more complicated or vague my quest, the more they seem to enjoy the challenge of tracking down just the right book or periodical. I spent many hours in a number of libraries around town appealing to these patient angels of information and I am deeply grateful to them all. Most particularly I want to thank Barbara Mathé and Ross Day at the Robert Goldwater Library in The Metropolitan Museum of Art for their cheerful attention to my "deathly" needs. Karen Nickeson at the Lincoln Center Library helped me solve a puzzling dilemma. My thanks as well to librarians at the Watson Library, also in the Metropolitan Museum; the librarians of the Donnell, Schomburg, St. Agnes, and Main Branches of the New York Public Library; and those at the Harlem Hospital Library. I am grateful to Rika Burnham in the Education Department of the Metropolitan Museum for her helpful research.

So many people have encouraged me along the way. Joyce Leung at Harlem Hospital was enthusiastic from the very start. My storytelling friend, Trudy Betcher, led me to "The Cow-Tail Switch." The Reverend Gary P. Fertig helped sort out the origins of "Ash Wednesday." James Hurtak came to my aid when I was mired down in sourcing ancient texts. My special thanks to Joan Buell, Toni Carey, Paul Matthews, and Dot Peters, who were kind enough to read and critique the manuscript as it developed. I appreciate their thoughtful comments and encouragement. Judy Leaf gave me extended bibliographies of folktales. Mark Rosenstein, who wept over some of the stories, was wonderfully sensitive in choosing music for the first *Some Folk Say* workshop. My thanks to Barry Keating and Pat Kery for listening and for supporting me along the way.

This book might still be languishing on editors' desks had not Sandy Wright whispered in my ear one evening as we gazed out over the glittering New York skyline, "Go for it!" It was at that moment that I took the plunge into the world of publishing. Throughout, Nina Resnick has been invaluable as my agent and counsel; her unwavering belief in this project has kept me going. Many thanks to Susan Converse Winslow for her wise and careful editing and helpful advice, also to Susan Moore for her precise line editing.

I am deeply grateful to Stéphan Daigle for his brilliant illustrations. His willingness to listen to my suggestions and adjust some of his early sketches was magnificent. We worked until we agreed that they fully satisfied the essence of the stories. What's more, I love his sense of humor. Another key player in this effort has been Julie Hill, my book designer and soon to become daughter-in-law. Not only has Julie led me patiently through the complexities of book publishing, but she shared my passion that this should be a *beautiful* book.

New York City, Summer, 1998

INTRODUCTION

Be careful then, and be gentle about death.
For it is hard to die, it is difficult to go through
the door, even when it opens.

—D. H. Lawrence, "All Soul's Day"

"Don't you find it depressing, researching and writing a book about death?" Variations of this question have been put to me a number of times in the past three years. My answer is always an emphatic, "Not at all!" The fact is, the further I explore the world of death stories, the more fascinated and excited I become by them, their deeper meanings, and the insights they might bring to anyone facing death, be it his own or that of a loved one. Sooner or later *everyone* has to deal with death.

For some children, the first experience of death and grieving comes with the death of a pet. How many dog, cat, gerbil, hamster, parakeet, and rabbit graves are there strewn across the land, I wonder? In the United States millions; in certain other parts of the world, none. In this country we often make elaborate monuments to our deceased loved ones, although we are ill prepared for their deaths or for the powerful feelings that emerge in death's wake.

Since we live in a society devoted to materialism, it is not surprising that the only preparation most people make for their death is to draw up a will to arrange for the disposition of their material goods. For many, even those decisions seem formidable.

Few spend time preparing for the spiritual transition involved in dying. Few really ask the fundamental questions: What, if anything, will happen after I die? Do I have a soul? If I have, what is to become of it when I die? How am I to approach death? How have I lived my life? Is there more than physical life?

These questions, in one form or another, may arise during a person's lifetime, but often they are pushed aside or ignored. Modern physical science cannot locate, weigh, or measure the soul, and it has no news for us about afterlife states or, indeed, about the purpose of the good life here on earth. Polls show that a large number of people do not believe in any kind of afterlife. It is no wonder, then, that they fear dying as an absolute end.

Starting in the late 60s, the subject of death and dying, banished so long from public discourse, has emerged from the shadows and become a topic of widespread interest. Dr. Elisabeth Kubler-Ross led the way with her classic, *On Death and Dying,* which has inspired millions and helped us understand the five stages of death. Her pioneering work brought the hospice movement to the United States thereby changing the way some people cope with the final chapter of life. Stephen Levine, in his many books such as *Healing into Life and Death* and *Who Dies?* writes about and works compassionately with the dying as well as the bereft. He and his wife, Ondrea, are tireless in their efforts to bring understanding and resolution to this population. A number of books on near-death experiences, some compiled by scientists, have become hugely popular. There are new translations of the ancient *The Tibetan Book of the Dead,* and now Sognol Rinpoche's 1993 *The Tibetan Book of Living and Dying* is prominently displayed in many bookstores. From this trend, we can guess that some people welcome evidence of life after death and hunger for information that could help them think about death in fresh ways.

The Purpose and Structure of This Book

The purpose of *Some Folk Say* is not so much to supply answers as to stimulate the imagination. By offering many different beliefs and practices regarding death and the afterlife, I hope the reader will want to explore the subject further rather than turn away from it in fear or denial. Consider this book as an invitation to renewed wonder, speculation, and reverie. As children, we all came endowed with these attributes; some of us need encouragement to reactivate them.

My imagination was stimulated when I read the section of William Buhlman's book, *Adventures Beyond the Body*, that deals with multidimensional universes. Citing the work of a number of modern physicists and mathematicians including Albert Einstein, Nathan Rosen, H. Reissner, G. Nordstrom, and others who have developed theories about "black holes" and "parallel universes," Buhlman suggests that these phenomena are in fact the nonmaterial realms known to mystics throughout the ages. Science, it seems, may at last have "discovered" heaven and hell. These other worlds universally described through story and art may actually exist as energy forms.[†] In a number of other ways modern science is validating ancient spiritual wisdom; perhaps here is yet another example of the merging of science and spirit. It is certainly something to think about as you wend your way through this collection.

Some Folk Say is not intended to be an anthology or even a full sampling of stories, myths, and poems dealing with death and the afterlife. Rather it is a personal selection of a few pieces chosen from a wealth of material that has been gathered by others. As the commentary suggests, I chose each piece for its unique quality and message. Some of the pieces are reprinted here just as I found them. Others, such as "The Green-Haired Giant," "Viraf's Vision," "The House of the Dead," The River," and "Gourd Woman" I have developed from brief descriptions or fragments from research material. My intention was to retain the general plot and message, while

---

[†] William Buhlman, *Adventures Beyond the Body: How to Experience Out-of-Body Travel* (HarperSanFrancisco, 1996) pp.75–127.

adding texture and color to bring the stories alive as they most certainly were in their original settings. In some of the stories about the afterlife, a problem arose early on that required adjusting the original material. The soul (as in "Gourd Woman") has no gender. Using "it" throughout, however, is awkward. I have given the soul a name and a gender, therefore, to help the reader identify with the protagonist. If I have strayed from the intended narrative, I beg forgiveness from my ancestral storytellers.

The book is divided into five sections, each addressing a different aspect of death and the afterlife. My hope is that these classifications will assist the reader rather than prove arbitrary or confusing. I have always had mixed feelings about putting things in boxes and applying labels. In my experience, the minute you decide anything belongs here and not there, it jumps out or slithers off or simply evaporates. The problem is, of course, that stories are not merely about one theme but often contain any number of themes and meanings. Different people may find different meanings in any given story; we bring our own sensing tools and reflectors with us when we enter the imaginal realms. If you find "Reconciliation" in a story in the section "After Death" or detect a "Lesson for Life" in the section "Origins of Death," so be it. Some people like to study in the dining room, eat in bed, and sleep in the study. Far be it from me to call them wrong. Please give yourself permission to make these offerings your own in any way that may serve.

STORIES OF COMFORT

In my search for stories about death and the afterlife from cultures around the world and throughout time, I was naturally attracted to those that felt comforting, that addressed some of my unspoken concerns, as well as the anguish and grief I have encountered in others. If, for instance, someone had read "The River" to me at age four and a half, as I struggled to cope with overwhelming sadness and confusion in the wake of my mother's death, would I have been comforted? I don't know, of course, but its simplicity, magic, and surprise ending are appealing.

In a similar way I felt drawn to "Coyote and Raven." The discussion in the beginning between Coyote and Raven reminds me of rambling conversations with my brothers and cousins when we were children. We would spend hours lolling about on beds staring at the ceiling or lying on the lawn chewing bits of grass while deciding just how we would arrange matters if we ruled the world. One such conversation, I seem to remember, took place underneath my aunt and uncle's four-poster. My cousin, Arthur, took the role of Raven, issuing edicts, while I played Coyote's part, asking the questions: What if, Yeah but why, and How come? As children, of course, we felt powerless to make the world bend to our will so we amused ourselves with imaginary all-powerful figures: "the Catchoo Man" and "Mr. Duz," who could do and fix anything.

The last part of "Coyote and Raven," was less comforting. Yet it still resonated with my experience, for it took me back to my first encounter with death. For many months after my mother's death, I dreamt about her. In one vivid dream I shall never forget, she came to me and wordlessly we made a deal that she would return and be with me, but I wouldn't be allowed to speak to her. In my dream I eagerly agreed to the bargain: When I awoke and realized I had been dreaming, I felt devastated. As I lay in my narrow cot in the corner of the nursery, I had to face the pain of no mother to hold my hand when we went out, to read me stories at bed time, to show me the way to be. How well I would have recognized Raven's anguished cry, "Do not let people die and remain dead forever. Let us change it!"

"Five Poppy Seeds" is yet another example of a story that can offer comfort, not that anything can change the reality of death; but to know that one is not alone in experiencing the agony of grief can be helpful. Is there anything more difficult to bear for a parent than the death of a child? Often one is at a loss to address such powerful grief. In times past when surviving into adulthood was not taken for granted, people expected death to take at least one of their children. Today in the Western world, we have very different expectations, and some parents never fully recover from the loss of a child. I know one mother who eventually took her own life, so distracted did she become and so unable to reconcile herself with her son's death. Would her pain have been eased had she read "Five Poppy Seeds" and taken the Buddha's teaching to heart?

Making the transition from the depths of despair brought on by the loss of a loved one to a place of acceptance is a vital step in coping with death. It is an essential journey, the path being different for each individual. A friend recently told me the following story. Several years ago her oldest son, Eric, died on his twenty-eighth birthday in a horrible, fiery automobile accident. She and he had been unusually close, and though a continent apart, each often knew when the other was needing to communicate and would telephone. For several months after Eric's death, whenever she drove in her car, she would talk to him, giving vent to her pain and grief. One day, as she drove off, she decided she wasn't going to do this any more so she said, "Eric, I'm not going to hang onto you any longer because I know you need to go, but, please may I have one last hug? I miss your hugs *so* much!" Immediately she felt herself enfolded in an unbelievably loving embrace. From that moment her torment lifted, and, like the mother in the Buddhist story, the raw pain of grief began to heal.

"The Spirit-Bride" speaks to the agony of losing a spouse or lover. So often the person left behind, like Running Deer in the story, feels compelled to join the beloved and has no will to go on living. When the couple are older and the bonds tightly woven, this sometimes indeed is what happens. In long-term relationships it is not uncommon for the surviving partner to languish and fail rapidly after the death of the beloved. And we have all heard of older people with devoted pets who die within days or weeks of one another. The magnetic pull of love is awesome. When the bereft lover is young and vigorous, however, the task parallels that of the Algonquin brave.

Other stories caught my attention by making me stop and think. They challenged my assumptions. Studying some of the ideas and practices of peoples and times very different from mine forced me to reflect on the cultural diversity surrounding me in daily life. "Gourd Woman" and "The Four Ways of Death" both fall into this category. The Kogi of Colombia are with us today and, like the Tibetans, their total commitment to an ancient spirituality and culture that counts each person's mortal life as but a chapter in a much larger and more challenging journey is compelling. Perhaps both groups might agree with J. M. Barrie's Peter Pan, who boasted that death is life's greatest adventure.

The Aztec, members of a warrior culture from the past, in "The Four Ways of Death," give us a glimpse into the point of view that to die for one's people is the highest honor one can achieve. It is interesting to note that Aztec women who died bringing new life into the world were similarly honored and, like the warrior, needed to struggle no more. Less honored but certainly pampered were those taken by phenomena beyond the control of human beings. Could it be that the very harshness of Aztec life gave rise to their system of benevolent life after death for these special categories of people?

Cultures throughout history have valued those who died defending others, be the "others" clan, tribe, cause, or nation. Our American culture today honors the slain warrior, as can be seen on countless plaques and monuments in their honor prominently placed on village greens, urban parks, and battlefields across the land. Do we believe, as the Aztec did, that these heros have an easier time of it in the afterlife?

As a child, how well I remember seeing those blue stars — one, two, three, and sometimes as many as four — sewn on little white banners edged in red with gold trim, hung in windows by proud mothers declaring to all the world, "My boys are serving their country!" World War II was the last "popular" war in U.S. history.

Today the attitude in this country is somewhat different; although many people still honor the military life, this commitment no longer includes "our boys" being killed. Ambivalence about warfare and the warrior's death has been with us, I suspect, throughout human history.

In Shakespeare's *Henry V*, for instance, on the night before the Battle of Agincourt, the English, greatly outnumbered by the "confident and over-lusty French," huddle around their campfires contemplating their almost certain death with the coming dawn. King Henry, disguised in the cloak of one of his officers, anonymously visits with some of his men as they ponder their fate. One of the soldiers, Williams, says:

> But if the cause be not good, the king himself hath a heavy reckoning to make when all those legs and arms and heads, chopped off in a battle, shall join together at the latter day and cry all, We died at such and such a place; some swearing; some crying for a surgeon; some upon their wives left poor behind them; some upon the debts they owe; some upon their children rawly left. I am afeared there are few that die well that die in a battle; for how can they charitably dispose of anything when blood is their argument? Now, if these men do not die well, it will be a black matter for the king that led them to it; who to disobey were against all proportion of subjection.

The disguised Henry counters this caution at length and concludes:

> Every subject's duty is the king's; but every subject's soul is his own. Therefore should every soldier in the wars do as every sick man in his bed,— wash every mote out of his conscience: and dying so, death is to him advantage; or not dying, the time was blessedly lost wherein such preparation was

gained: and in him that escapes it were not sin to think that, making God so free an offer, he let him outlive that day to see his greatness, and to teach others how they should prepare.

Henry is able to send his subjects into battle, to die if necessary, because he does *not* take responsibility for their souls but considers the soul a private matter between the individual soldier and God. The Aztec warrior went off to war ingrained with the belief that, should he die in battle, his struggles would be over, because an honored future was assured. In both instances, the philosophy appears to justify the action. If this reasoning be true for warriors, what of women?

In the twentieth century, women in the developed world have achieved some success in their efforts to break away from the traditional, deeply held belief that their only appropriate career is motherhood. Much of the world, however, still believes bearing children to be women's primary role. The death of a mother in childbirth is universally mourned by her family. Yet society at large ignores it. There are no plaques or monuments to such women, no holidays declared, no parades or speeches. Whatever our private attitudes may be about women, their role in society, the importance of motherhood, I know of no group today that honors the souls of women taken in childbirth as the Aztec did. Yes, "The Four Ways of Death" gave me much to think about. When I first encountered it, it was as though I had taken a stick and poked it into the still pond of my collected assumptions. All sorts of unsuspected material rose up from the bottom and caught my attention.

STORIES BEYOND COMPREHENSION

Finally it seemed important to honor stories that represent beliefs beyond my grasp to comprehend, just as there are individuals today whose death stories are shocking or bizarre. "The Death of Great Sun," Father le Petit's eyewitness account of the Natchez's mortuary rites, is included because, uncomfortable as it may be to contemplate, it describes behavior and attitudes about death and the afterlife that have been with us for millennia. Distressing variations of this phenomenon continue to confront us today in mass suicides such as those of the Branch Davidians in Waco, Texas, in 1993, the Jones group in Guyana, South America, fifteen years earlier; and the Heaven's Gate group in California in 1997. The point is not to condemn or condone such behavior but rather to note it as a recurring theme in human belief and behavior concerning death.

COMMON THREADS

Even though the stories in this collection are but a tiny sampling from cultures rich in legend and myth on a variety of topics, I notice a common thread running through many of them — their view of the afterlife reflects their life on earth. The Tlingit, for instance, living in a harsh, cold climate, face possible death every day in their struggle to survive. The story they tell one another of what will happen after death is of being reborn and reunited with loved ones at the end of their journey: It is a tale of reassurance. The warlike Aztec, as noted, believe the slain warrior will be honored in the heavens, a powerful aid to those heading into battle. The Kogi's after-death story, while stressing personal accountability, couples it with compassion in the form of Gourd Woman, who never deserts the soul during its journey and is always present as a supporting influence. This relationship mirrors what I understand of the Kogi way of life, which respects lifelong discipline and personal responsibility, while at the same time supporting and caring for all of its members; no one in the Kogi world is ever cast out or abandoned. The Origin of Death story "The Cast-Off Skin" delivers a message of conciliation and accommodation in answer to the query, "Why death?" "Coyote and Raven" answers the same question very differently: Once a decision is made, it cannot be changed. If one were to investigate the two cultures from which these stories come, one would find quite different lifestyles. Traditional life in the South Pacific, where the weather is habitually warm and food was plentiful, tended to be slow paced and nonconfrontational; whereas Native Americans of the Pacific Northwest had to contend with the harsh realities of severe weather and a more aggressive way of life. Thus the stories they tell one another about death reflect this difference.

To take another example, the philosophy of the Pueblo Indians of Taos as expressed in "Song of the Hunter" is one of humans forming part of the cycle of all life in which death is not only a natural but necessary element. A chance encounter with a member of the Taos pueblo a few years ago left an indelible impression on me. On my second visit to that historic community, I struck up a conversation with a man behind the counter in one of the little shops. I was immediately drawn to his quiet strength, which combined simple humility with a distinct self-assurance. In the course of our exchange, he revealed that he was the chief of his people, minding the shop for his daughter-in-law! He confessed to being amused at finding himself in this role. Here, it seemed, was a part of the Taos philosophy made manifest: To lead is to serve; to live is to take life; to die is to give life.

The more I immersed myself in "death stories," the more I came to understand that the manner in which people live out their lives depends in large part on what they believe will happen to them after they die, *even when these beliefs lie hidden in the shadow of unawareness.*

The Institute for the Study of the Afterdeath, (ISA) conducted a poll of religious and spiritual leaders around the world in 1994. ISA reported, "There is 90 percent agreement among groups studied that the afterdeath journey is transformational, that it leads to a specific place and that it ends with a return to life." It is not surprising to find such a high degree of consensus from religious and spiritual leaders regarding what happens when a person dies. If, however, ISA were to interview ordinary people on the streets of cities and towns across the United

States, they might encounter a greater degree of doubt, cynicism, despair, and even ignorance regarding the after-death experience.[†]

Could it be that American society's current obsession with materialism and consumerism has its roots in a commonly held but often unexpressed belief that there is no life after death: This is it? Or is it the other way around? Does the lack of any belief in an afterlife arise from our materialism? Either way, what seems apparent is that the manner in which people live their lives is inextricably linked with what they believe will happen after they die.

The American playwright Thornton Wilder may have another piece to add to this puzzling question: What is the meaning of death and by extension, of life? I was first exposed to Wilder's great twentieth-century classic, *Our Town*, when we performed it in high school. The play depicts life in rural Grover's Corners, New Hampshire, during the first part of this century. Deceptively simple in style, the action takes place on a bare stage with only a few chairs, stools, and ladders as props. Throughout, a character called the Stage Manager (a stand-in for Wilder) describes each scene, introduces the players, sets up the action, and interjects homespun philosophy. Much of that philosophy has stayed with me over the years. One bit seems relevant here.

At the beginning of the third act, where the setting is a hilltop graveyard, the Stage Manager stands looking at the graves (actually chairs) filled with some of the people we have come to know in the first two acts. He sets the date as 1913 and describes some of the changes that have taken place in Grover's Corners during the decade since the start of the play. Then he takes up his philosopher's stance, as he suggests that everyone knows, perhaps subconsciously, that "something is eternal" about life. Clearly it isn't any of the material things surrounding us on earth and not even the stars. Foremost thinkers have told us about our eternal nature, he says, but

---

[†] Sukie Miller, "Beliefs About the Afterdeath: Survey of IONS Members," *Noetic Sciences Bulletin*, Autumn, 1994. p.8–9.

we keep forgetting. The dead lose their concern for the living after awhile, he continues; they disengage from human affairs. He asks the audience: Aren't the recently deceased in a kind of holding pattern, waiting for "the eternal part in them" to emerge?

As you wend your way through this collection, you might want to allow Wilder's question to accompany you. In an odd way, so many of the stories people have told one another about death and the afterlife are connected to that question: What is lasting, what is eternal?

The recent explosion of books about death, near-death experiences, and the afterlife indicates a yearning for a more compelling story than the statement "There is no life after death: This is it." Perhaps this sudden popular interest in death is a reaction to the undercurrent of helplessness, despair, and consequent cynicism pervading a society addicted to materialism and high-tech solutions for every dilemma. Technology can be a wonderful tool in a million ways, but ultimately it cannot defeat death. Are we, I wonder, in the process of crafting our new afterlife story? I like to believe we have not lost our capacity to envision or our affinity for storytelling.

ORIGINS OF DEATH

Death is different from what anyone knows, and luckier.

Leaves of Grass   WALT WHITMAN

So often when someone we know dies we form the question, whether silently or vocally, Why did she have to die? Why did he die now? Behind these anguished laments lies hidden a more fundamental query, Why death? People have been struggling with that question, I suspect, since we became conscious human beings. As children we are outraged when that which we love is taken from us; reasoning does little to assuage our distress. Death, particularly an unexpected death, can bring out that childlike response in the most sophisticated adult.

The stories in this section address that basic need to grapple with the concept of death itself. Almost every known culture has stories dealing with the origin of death. Perhaps the most familiar in Western culture is the story of Adam and Eve in the Garden of Eden. The ones chosen here are a small sampling of the countless attempts to plumb one of the deepest mysteries: Why Death?

The Argument

Native American: The Coeur d'Alene of northern Idaho

Once there was a woman who had two children, a brother and sister, who suddenly fainted dead away. When she discovered them like this, the woman was greatly alarmed, but, she said, "Possibly they are only sleeping. I will not disturb them but let them rest." The next morning their mother left them and when she returned in the evening, they were still lying there. However, she noticed fresh tracks like theirs around the house. "They must have come to life and played while I was away," she reasoned. "Perhaps I have nothing to worry about after all." This continued day after day; whenever she returned home the children were asleep, but there were always fresh signs of their having been active.

Finally she became so consumed with curiosity, she decided to take action. One day she returned home at midday and stole in on them unseen. She found the children arguing with each other inside the lodge. One said, "It is better to be dead." The other said, "It is better to be alive." When they saw her, they stopped talking; and since then people die from time to time, always some living ones and some dead ones. Had she remained hidden, and allowed them to finish their argument, one would have prevailed over the other, and there would have been either no life or no death.

"Origin of Death," in *Folk Tales of Salishan and Sahaptin Tribes,* edited by Franz Boas, p.125 (New York: The American Folk-Lore Society, 1917, Kraus Reprint Co., 1969). Permission applied for.

Many aboriginal groups, particularly in Oceanic cultures, have origin-of-death stories involving an argument, a mistake, or an act of disobedience. The familiar Adam and Eve story found in Genesis would come under the heading of a disobedience version of the origin of death.

"The Argument" can make us ask an unusual question: What if life and death did not alternate, but there were only one or the other? If there were only life, we would face the problem of Tithonus, the Greek gentleman who asked for eternal life but forgot to add a provision for eternal youth and so grew horribly old and infirm until released from suffering by the gods. That story reminds us of the need for death — as relief, as release. And if only death existed — no life at all — then we would not be here asking the questions.

Coyote and Raven

Native American: The Salishan of British Columbia

Coyote traveled until he met Raven, a bad, selfish chief. Raven wanted to make everything difficult for other people, and easy for himself. He wanted all the game for himself, wanted long winters, and he did not want man to be immortal.

Coyote questioned him as to why he wanted people to die.

Raven said, "If people were immortal, there would be too many. Let them become sick and die."

Coyote said, "Why should they die? Death will introduce sorrow into the world and sorrow is very hard. If they die, what will become of them? Where will they go? Let them be sick but not die."

Raven said, "No, they must die. I do not want our enemies to live forever. If the people should become too numerous, there would be no food, and they would be hungry. It is better for them to die."

Raven's people supported their chief and clamored for human beings to die. Raven, Crow, Fly, Maggot, and many others wanted people to die, so that they might feed on the corpses.

Coyote said, "Let people die for a while, and then come to life again. Let death be like sleep."

Raven said, "No, if they die, let them die for good, and let their bodies rot."

"Origin of Death," collected by James A. Tait, in *Folk-Tales of Shalisan and Sahaptin Tribes*, edited by Franz Boas, p. 1 (New York: The American Folk-Lore Society, 1917, Kraus Reprint Co., 1969). Permission applied for.

At last Coyote agreed and said, "Well, it is ordained that people shall die when their time has come. Their bodies shall be buried, and their souls shall go to the spirit-land; but this will only be until the world changes again, when they will die no more."

Shortly after that, Raven's daughter became sick and died. She was the first to die. Raven tried to restore her to life but failed. Then he wept because of his daughter. He went to Coyote and said, "Let us change what we said before. Do not let people die and remain dead forever. Let us change it!"

Coyote answered, "No, it is settled now and cannot be altered." Thus it happens that people die and are buried.

Coyote and Raven figure in many Native American stories from a wide variety of tribes. While Coyote often plays the role of the trickster, he regularly acts as a divine authority figure delivering judgments and declaring universal truths.

Native Americans, though diverse in many ways, shared one quality; they all possessed a rich collection of stories that were told over and over to help instill and pass on their understanding of what today we might call ethics and spirituality. For them, the stories were not incidental, but central to every aspect of their daily life. Like all indigenous people, their stories formed the basis of their entire culture. Although much of this rich oral heritage was brutally expunged and lost after the coming of Europeans, many of the stories continued to be passed down through generation after generation. Today not only are some Native Americans returning to appreciate the ways of their forebears, but also descendants of those earlier "Indian killers" are discovering the subtle wisdom of Native American spirituality.

This story holds some difficult truths. Coyote tries to bargain with Raven, first for only sickness, then for only temporary death ("Let people die for a while, and then come to life again"). Later, though he allows death to come, he still decrees that it will not be altogether final: "This will only be until the world changes." If Coyote has some power to ease human fate, why not all power? Why must he give Raven so much? Why can't he change things back when Raven repents?

Whatever our beliefs about a protective God, God has not ordered the universe so as to protect us from heartbreak. Though we may all come to life again when "the world changes," that possibility seems remote and holds little comfort for those, who like Raven are caught up in the immediate grief for the loss of a loved one.

The Cast-Off Skin

Melanesian: Banks Islands, northeast of Australia

Some folk say that in the beginning, people did not die. Rather they cast their skins like snakes and crabs, and thus renewed their youth.

One day, an old woman noticed that her skin had become wrinkled and worn. In some places it was discolored and in others calloused and hard. What's more, her hair was dull and sparse. "This will never do," she thought to herself. "I've been so absorbed in my work, I didn't realize what was happening to me." So she stopped what she was doing and went to a nearby stream to change her skin. She wriggled and hopped about until the old wrinkled skin was released and fell to the ground. Then she picked it up and cast it into the stream, where it floated away. The woman, now transformed into a beautiful young girl with glowing skin and shining hair, watched the old skin drift down stream until it was almost out of sight around a bend. Just as she turned around to head back to her village, the skin caught on a stick lodged in the mud near the bank.

When the woman returned home, her little daughter refused to recognize her in her new and youthful form. So upset was the child that she sobbed without ceasing day and night. "Alas, what am I to do?" cried the woman. "I cannot bear to see my child so distraught!" She thought and thought, her daughter's wails ringing in her ears. Finally she made up her mind. "I must return to the stream to search for my old

Adapted from material in *The Mythology of All Races*, vol. IX, *Oceanic*, Roland B. Dixon, p. 118. (Boston: Marshall Jones Co., 1916). Reprinted with permission of Marshall Jones Company, ©1916.

skin," she said to herself. So the woman retraced her steps to the spot where she had cast off her old skin. But her heart was heavy for she was sure the skin was far downstream by now and she had little hope of ever finding it. Nevertheless, she walked along the bank, searching carefully in every eddy. As she rounded a bend, there she saw the discarded skin stuck on the stick not far from shore. With a cry of delight, she waded into the water, carefully detached the old skin from the stick, and carried it to shore, where she dried it off and then stepped back into her familiar form. "So," she declared, "My child will stop crying and be happy once more. Everyone will recognize me now!"

From that time people have ceased to cast their skins and have died when they grew old.

For whose sake must we die? If not for our own, then surely for our children's. It is said that a wise man was called to the court of the emperor and asked to say a blessing. He said, "Grandfather dies, father dies, child dies." The emperor was horrified at this apparent curse and indignantly demanded some explanation. The wise man replied that he wished the very best for the emperor and his family. "It is in the way of things for the older to die so that the young can take over for them. No greater calamity can befall a dynasty than for the generations to die out of order, with the child departing before the parent." The emperor had to acknowledge the wisdom of this statement, and he humbly thanked the wise man for his reminder that, after all, death must come and do its work of pruning and clearing.

The people of the Banks Islands, from whence this story comes, believed that in the beginning men lived forever, casting their skins, and that the permanent retention of property in the same hands led to much trouble. How different this origin-of-death story is from those that suggest an argument, a mistake, or punishment for wrongdoing as the cause. The old woman is willing to give up her life to avoid upsetting her daughter. This attitude bespeaks a culture that respects a continuity of identity with the next generation, not clinging to this body's eternal perfection but finding one's joy in one's children's flourishing.

The Green-Haired Giant

African: The Togo of West Africa

People tell about a time of great famine, when a boy named Wattu was searching in the forest for something to eat. Suddenly he came upon a strangely shaped great rock, which as he examined it, looked like the head of a sleeping giant. Cascading from the rock were long, strong forest vines that resembled green hair. "That's curious," thought Wattu "I must remember to tell my family about this when I get home." The boy walked a little farther and then tripped over what he thought was a vine. As he picked himself up, he heard rustling sounds behind him and turned to discover the vine he had trod on was attached to the head of a real, live giant! As Wattu watched spellbound, the giant slowly awoke, propped himself on one elbow while he rubbed his eyes with his hand, and then, gathering his legs under him, gradually stood up. The boy looked up and saw the giant staring down at him from such a height that his head and shoulders towered above the trees.

Oddly Wattu was not frightened but asked, "Please, sir, do you have any food? I haven't eaten in days and I am very hungry." The giant said nothing but continued to stare down at the boy while he reached a huge hand the size of a tree stump into a pouch hanging from his waist and pulled out some dried meat. Stooping down, he handed it to Wattu. "Oh, thank you, thank you, sir!" piped Wattu as he took the meat and eagerly began to devour it on the spot. From his lofty height, the giant continued

Adapted from material in *Myths of Life & Death*, by C.A. Burland, pp.241–242 (New York: Crown Publishers, ©1974). Used with permission.

to observe Wattu. Finally he spoke, his words sounding like rolling thunder. "What is your name, boy?"

"Wattu, sir," replied the boy between bites, "People call me Wattu."

"Very well, Wattu," boomed the giant. "You shall come home with me where you can make yourself useful as my servant." Wattu stopped chewing and his eyes opened wide. "In return I shall see to it that you enjoy all you can eat in the way of succulent fresh meat. What say you to that, my boy?" Wattu was overjoyed at his sudden good fortune and agreed to be the giant's servant and live in his house. For a long time all went well.

One day as Wattu was sweeping the giant's house, he became aware of a gnawing empty feeling in his heart and a strange heaviness in his limbs. His mind kept returning to his family and his village. Wattu longed to hear his mother's voice, to play with his brothers and sisters, and to feel his father's presence as they sat together in the evenings. As he thought about these things, Wattu became sadder and sadder. Finally he went to the giant and asked, "Please, Master, I am so grateful for all you have given me, but I have a great sadness in my heart and long to see my family once more. Please may I return to my village so that I may visit with my people and know they are all well?"

Wattu had been a faithful and hard-working servant, so the giant told him he could go home, provided he brought his brother back to take his place. Wattu gladly agreed. With his spirits restored, he raced home to his village, brought his brother back to the giant's house, and then went home once again to stay there for a time. When Wattu finally returned to the giant's house, his brother was not there. The giant told him he had sent the lad off to a far country on an errand. " Aha," thought

Wattu, "my brother must have served my master well to be trusted on such an important mission to a far-off land." So Wattu settled back into performing his routine duties and all was well. The giant and Wattu ate good meat, and many people settled near them, forming a village. Wattu was content enough for a time, but after a while his longing to see his family returned. Once more he went to the giant and asked permission to visit his people.

Once more the giant agreed and made Wattu promise to bring a helper back with him; this time it was to be his sister. "One arm is bent since birth, Master, but she's a very good worker," promised Wattu. So the boy brought her to the giant, where she remained while he returned for a visit with his parents.

When Wattu came back to the giant's place, his sister was nowhere to be seen. The giant, in response to the boy's query, said, "Do not be concerned, lad. I have sent her on a special mission to fetch a gourd of the purest water from a distant mountain lake." Wattu was given more fresh, sweet meat; it was delicious and he was happy. So once more he busied himself with work. One day, when the giant was resting in an enormous hammock slung between two huge trees near the house, Wattu approached and asked him for another meal. The giant, who was feeling well content and very drowsy, muttered, "Yes, yes! Go to the storehouse yourself and fetch whatever you like." Wattu was surprised at this, because heretofore the giant alone went into the storehouse. He took the giant at his word, however, and entered the dark, cool room. There he lit a torch and saw the meat neatly laid out and beside it a little pile of fresh bones. Among them was an armbone with a slight deformity. Horrified, Wattu recognized it as his sister's arm! So Death had been feeding him on his own relatives. Now he saw that the giant was Death, an ogre living on human flesh. Wattu rushed out the door and raced as never before to the village to tell his lurid story.

The villagers agreed; the land must be purged of this evil monster, so they hastily conferred and hatched a plan. They waited till night, when the giant was sleeping, and then, led by Wattu, they set fire to the giant's house. The giant slept on, merely tossing and turning as the flames surrounded him. Then the house fell in, and the giant was dead, completely burned up except for his head. As he crept closer through the smoldering embers, Wattu spied a leaf-packet of powder nestled in the giant's green hair. Wattu remembered hearing from the elders of his village that there was supposed to be a powder that could bring back the dead.

Wasting no time, Wattu grabbed the leaf-packet and put some powder on his sister's arm bone. Suddenly there she stood, just as delightful as when she was alive! Then he found some more bones, put powder on them, and instantly there was his brother! More bones, more powder, and other children appeared. It seemed miraculous and everyone was happy. But Wattu was curious and threw a little powder at the giant's head. It fell on the eye.

At that very moment someone in the crowd cried out, "Look! The giant just blinked!" Everyone turned to stare at the giant's head. Sure enough, the green eye was slowly opening! Just at that moment, the person standing closest to the head slumped to the ground — dead. The people all ran away.

Ever since then, when the eye of Death glances at a human being, that person dies. In fact, every day, somewhere in the world a person dies and people don't know why. It is merely that Death has looked upon him.

Many cultures have stories of children being eaten by giants, witches, or other creatures representing death. In the familiar European "Hansel and Gretel," the children are saved from death by their own cleverness, and the witch (death) is killed. In this African story, death is not vanquished but given a place in the over-all scheme.

The great moments in life come when we focus our attention; death comes when something else focuses its attention on us. We can talk about death abstractly — such talk is cheap — but there are moments when among mortals, discussions of death become real, immediate, vital. It is not so much that our words touch on it, but rather that death touches us. Can we bear that touch? Can we, in terms of this story, bear its green gaze?

Silently the tree opened its trunk just enough for the terrified Garo to creep inside.

The Two White Pigs

Melanesian: Admiralty Islands, north of New Guinea

Once there was a man named Garo, who set off in his canoe to fish. While he was out on the water, an evil spirit came to him and declared, "Garo, I have come to kill and eat you! You cannot escape from my power!" So terrified was Garo of the evil spirit that he paddled as he had never paddled before toward shore, and as his boat touched land, he leapt out and raced into the forest for protection.

He ran until he came to a giant tree. Enveloping the trunk with his outstretched arms, Garo pleaded, "Oh, Great Tree, protect me from an evil spirit who is pursuing me, who vows to kill and eat me!" The tree looked down at the trembling figure at its feet and took pity. Silently the tree opened its trunk just enough for the terrified Garo to creep inside. Then the trunk closed again without a sound. Presently the evil spirit came wandering through the forest looking for Garo, but finding him nowhere, it eventually gave up and departed.

The Great Tree opened once more, and Garo stepped out. "How can I repay you for saving my life?" he asked.

"Bring me two white pigs," replied the great tree. So Garo went home to his village to fetch two white pigs. White pigs, being extremely rare, were hard to come by. Garo figured he could cheat the great tree, who would be none the wiser, so he

Adapted from material in *The Mythology of All Races*, vol. 9, *Oceanic*, by Roland B. Dixon, p.119 (Boston: Marshall Jones Co., 1916). Reprinted with permission of Marshall Jones Company, ©1916.

returned with what appeared to be two white pigs. Only one was truly white, however; the other being black whitened with chalk.

"Here are the two white pigs, Great Tree," said Garo, as he stood shuffling uncomfortably from one foot to the other. The Great Tree reached out a branch and touched the back of the whitened black pig, revealing a streak of black beneath the chalk.

"You are unthankful, though I was good to you," he rebuked Garo. "If you had done what I had asked, you might have taken refuge in me whenever danger threatened. Now you cannot, but must die." So, as a result of man's ingratitude, the human race is doomed to mortality and cannot escape the enmity of evil spirits.

Perhaps to avoid a universe of senseless and malevolent power, many stories suggest that death has taken hold because of our own actions. Here it is man's untruthfulness for the sake of personal gain that results in the institution of death. The evil spirit did not have the power on its own to impose its will on the human being. Nor did the tree capriciously refuse its loyal protection. Rather, it was man himself who betrayed the order of things. He himself is responsible for transforming the gentle oscillation between moving about in the open and hiding in the tree trunk, into the harsh alternation of life and death.

In the healthy order of things, man is in nature, participating in its vitality. When he wants to grab a private realm for himself — by lying — he withdraws from nature and so loses that vitality.

BALANCING LIFE
AND DEATH

*[People] die in the morning, they are born in the evening,
like foam on the water.*

KOMO NO CHOMEI

The term balancing is used for this group of stories because each one deals with alternative possibilities. How do we balance life and death? How does death keep life in balance? Here again the stories are addressing the great mysteries behind the forces of power, pattern, and intention. Death often throws us off balance and we long to return to equilibrium. By the same token, we say life "throws us a curve." By this we mean, we have been caught off balance by unexpected events or the unexpected consequences of our actions. The stories in this section are offered as a kind of seesaw with a movable fulcrum upon which the reader may explore various points of balance.

The Quiver of Arrows

Ancient Greek: Aesop

It was a hot sultry summer afternoon, and Eros, tired with play and faint from the heat, took shelter in a cool, dark cave. It happened to be the cave of Death himself.

Eros, wanting only to rest, threw himself down carelessly — so carelessly that all his arrows fell out of his quiver.

When he awoke, he found they had mingled with the arrows of Death, which also lay scattered about the floor of the cave. They were so alike Eros could not tell the difference. He knew, however, how many had been in his quiver and eventually he gathered up the right amount.

Of course, Eros took some that belonged to Death and left some of his own behind.

And so it is today that we often see the hearts of the old and the dying struck by bolts of Love; and sometimes we see the hearts of the young captured by Death.

"Eros and Death," reworked by Steve Sanfield, a fable by Aesop in *Death: An Anthology of Ancient Texts, Songs, Prayers & Stories*, edited by David Meltzer, p.72 (San Francisco: North Point Press, 1984). Used with permission.

This story and "The Green-Haired Giant" are examples of ways in which people have explained the inexplicable; have answered the cries of loved ones, "Why did she have to die?" or "What a terrible waste: He was so young!" They suggest a parallel between two kinds of self-loss: losing oneself in the beloved and losing oneself in death. It is easy for us to see love as a kind of death — the Elizabethans referred to orgasm as "dying" — but harder to see physical death as an act of love. Many, if not most, deaths are not clearly loving, transcendent, or peaceful events as far as one can see. But that may not be very far. What matters in the end is not to evaluate others but to wonder about our own immediate experience. Can we rediscover the connection between dying and love in our lives?

Often we become stuck in the grieving process because we cannot accept the reality of the loss, especially when the person is young. As with all our experience, not just that concerning death, our minds keep searching for reasons, explanations. We crave understanding. In "The Quiver of Arrows," Aesop gives us an explanation for the death of a young person. If we can accept it, perhaps the raw pain of grief can subside and we can begin to heal.

The Moon's Message

African: The Hottentots of South Africa

They say that once upon a time, the Moon sent an insect to men, saying, "Go to men and tell them, 'As I die and dying live, so you shall also die and dying live!'"

The insect started off with the message, but as it was going on its way it was overtaken by the hare, who asked, "Where are you going?"

The insect answered, "The Moon has sent me as a messenger to men, to tell them that as she dies and dying lives, so shall they also die and dying live."

The hare said, "As you are a slow and awkward runner, let me go." With these words he ran off and when he came to the place where men lived, he said, "I am sent by the Moon to tell you, 'As I die and wholly perish, in the same way you also shall die and come to an end.'"

The hare then returned to the Moon and told her what he had said to men. The Moon scolded him, saying, "Do you dare to tell the people a thing which I have not said?"

With these words the Moon picked up a piece of wood and struck the hare on the nose. Since that day the hare's nose has been split, but the men still believe what he told them.

In *Myths and Legends of Africa*, by Margaret Carey, pp. 8–9 (London: Hamlyn, a division of Reed Consumer Books, Ltd. 1970). Used with permission.

The Hottentots of southern Africa, along with the Bushmen, are believed to be among the oldest surviving African people. Their physical appearance (their skin is a golden brown) and their language (characterized by "clicks") are distinctive. How many thousands of years do you suppose they have gathered around their small fires, looked up at the moon, and told this tale?

There is a theme of rebirth in the moon's message: It wanes and disappears but then waxes and lives again. At another level, the moon asserts that life inheres in the process of dying itself. Mother Theresa's Missionaries of Charity daily repeat St. Francis's prayer, which ends, "It is by dying that we are born again to eternal life."

A story from New Zealand has the moon cast in a different role. "Maui wished that man might not die forever, and so said to Hina, the moon, 'Let death be very short — that is, let man die and live again, and live on forever,' where-upon Hina replied, 'Let death be very long, that man may sigh and sorrow.' Maui again said, 'Let man die and live again, as you, the moon, die and live again,' but Hina said, 'No, let men die and become like soil, and never rise to life again.' And so it was."[†]

[†] Dixon, Roland B., *The Mythology of All Races,* vol. 9, *Oceanic* (Boston: Marshall Jones Co., 1916), p. 54. Used with permission.

Godfather Death

German: Grimm Brothers

A poor man had twelve children and had to work day and night just to keep them in bread. When the thirteenth came into the world, he didn't know what on earth to do and went out on the great highway intending to ask the first man he met to be sponsor. The first man he met was the good Lord God, who already knew what was weighing on his mind and said to him, "Poor man, I'm sorry for you; I'll stand sponsor for your child, care for it, and make it happy on Earth."

"Who are you?" said the man.

"I'm the good Lord."

"Then I don't want you as godfather," said the man. "You give to the rich and let the poor starve." The man said this because he didn't know how wisely God distributes wealth and poverty. So he turned away from the Lord and went on.

Then the Devil approached him and said, "What are you looking for? If you'll have me as sponsor for your child, I'll give him gold aplenty and all the joys of the World besides."

"Who are you?" asked the man.

"I'm the Devil."

"Then I don't want you as a sponsor; you deceive men and lead them astray," said the man and went on.

In *The Grimms German Folk Tales*, translated by Francis P. Magoun, Jr. and Alexander H. Krappe, pp. 158–160 (Carbondale: Southern Illinois University Press, 1960). Copyright ©1960 by Southern Illinois Press. Used with permission.

Then withered Death stepped up to him and said, "Take me as a sponsor."

"Who are you?" asked the man.

"I'm Death, who makes all men equal."

Then the man said, "You're the right person. You fetch rich and poor alike without distinction. You shall act as sponsor for me."

"I'll make your child rich and famous," answered Death, "for whoever has me for a friend can't but prosper."

The man said, "The christening's next Sunday. Be there on time." Death appeared as he'd promised and made a thoroughly proper godfather.

When the boy grew up, his godfather appeared one day and bade him come with him. He led him out into the forest and, showing him an herb growing there, said, "Now you're to receive your christening present. I'm making you a famous physician. When you're summoned to a sick person, I'll appear every time. If I'm standing at the sick man's head, you may speak up boldly, and say that you'll cure him. Then give him some of the herb, and he'll get well. But if I'm standing at the sick man's feet, he's mine and you must say that nothing can be done and that no physician in the world can save him. Beware of using the herb against my will or it might fare ill with you."

It wasn't long before the youth was the most famous physician in the whole world. "He has only to look at a patient and he already knows how things stand: whether he'll get well or is doomed to die." Such was his reputation and people came from far and near, brought him to the sick, and gave him so much money that he was soon a rich man.

Now it happened that the king fell ill. The physician was summoned and was supposed to say whether recovery was possible. As he approached the bed, Death was standing at the sick man's feet, and so there was no herb that could cure him. "If I could outwit Death just once!" thought the physician, "Of course he'll take it amiss, but since I'm his godchild, he'll surely let it pass. I'll risk it." Accordingly, he took the sick man and turned him the other way about, so that Death was now standing at his head. Then he gave him some of the herb, and the king recovered and got well again.

Death, however, came to the physician and with dark and angry looks shook his finger at him, saying, "You tricked me! This time I'll excuse you, because you're my godchild, but if you dare do it again, you'll catch it, and I'll carry you yourself off with me."

Soon after, the king's daughter fell seriously ill; she was his only child. He wept day and night until his eyes got blind and he had it proclaimed that whoever saved her from death should be her husband and inherit the crown. When the physician came to the sick girl's bed, he saw Death at her feet. He should have remembered his godfather's warning, but the great beauty of the king's daughter and the advantage of becoming her husband so deluded him that he threw all discretion to the winds. He didn't see that Death was looking at him angrily, that he was raising his hand and shaking his fist at him. He picked up the sick girl and put her head where her feet had been. Then he administered the herb to her, and forthwith her cheeks got rosy and life stirred anew.

When Death saw himself cheated out of his own for a second time, he strode up to the physician and said, "You're done for, and now it's your turn," seized him with his icy hand so hard that he couldn't resist, and led him into an underground cavern. There he saw thousands upon thousands of candles burning in endless rows, some large, some medium, others small. Every moment some went out and others flared up again, so the flames seemed to be perpetually hopping about hither and thither. "You see," said Death, "these are the life candles of men. The big candles belong to children, the medium-sized to married people in the prime of life, the small to the aged. But children and small people, too, often have just a small candle."

"Show me my life candle," said the physician, supposing it would still be quite big.

Death pointed to a tiny stub that was just threatening to go out and said, "You see, there it is."

"Oh, dear Godfather," said the frightened physician, "light a fresh candle for me. Do it as a favor so I may enjoy my life, become king and the husband of the king's beautiful daughter."

"I can't," answered Death. "One candle must go out before a new one starts to burn."

"Then put the old one on the new, which will go right on burning when the old one is used up," begged the physician. Death pretended that he was going to grant him his wish and fetched a big new candle, but because he wanted to revenge himself, he blundered on purpose in putting the fresh one on and the stub tipped over and went out. At once the physician dropped to the ground, he himself had now fallen into the hands of Death.

The most telling line in this story, perhaps, is Death's remark, "Whoever has me for a friend can't but prosper." Presumably we are not afraid of our friends and don't try to cheat them. Friendship, after all, is built on trust. The famous physician, however, loses sight of this truth and makes Death his enemy, so focused is he on his own desires and ambitions. Perhaps it is worth considering this thought: What kind of world might we have if people were truly able to make death their friend?

Song of the Hunter

Native American: The Pueblo Indians of Taos, New Mexico

I have killed the deer.

I have crushed the grasshopper

And the plants he feeds upon.

I have cut through the heart

Of trees growing old and straight.

I have taken fish from water

And birds from the sky.

In my life I have needed death

So that my life can be.

When I die I must give life

To what has nourished me.

The earth receives my body

And gives it to the plants

And to the caterpillars

To the birds

And to the coyotes

Each in its own turn so that

The circle of life is never broken.

In *Hollering Sun*, by Nancy Wood, (New York: Simon & Schuster, 1972). Used with permission.

When I die I must give life
To what has nourished me.

The Pueblo Indians of Taos, New Mexico, continue to maintain their tightly knit traditional pueblo life in spite of centuries of persecution from outsiders. Like the people of other intensely spiritual cultures, the Taos Indians believe all life is sacred. They see humans as part of nature, not above it ("These are our brothers: all men and all animals and all trees") and therefore strive to do no harm.

Implied in "Song of the Hunter" is the notion that all life, not just physical existence, but life on other planes as well, is essentially in the service of others. Just as we need to take life in order to live, so we give our life to support others. Death then is seen as one gift in a cycle.

A story came to me recently of the death of a man in his early forties after a long bout with cancer. The storyteller was well acquainted with death having been an intensive care nurse for many years.

"Brad and his wife, Donna, were shepherds. They came to Eastern Maine eighteen years ago from Southern California. Donna never wears shoes; they slept outdoors in the winter, always gave away food. Whatever Brad had, he would give. In the final days several of us took turns sitting with him in their log cabin so he was never alone.

"A few days before he died, Donna and a crew took their boat and went out to fetch the lambs off the island before winter set in. Brad was still conscious, aware of their activities, and excited to have the work go forward. It was a gorgeous sunny day, rare for November. They brought the lambs back to the farm and began the three-day process of slaughtering, skinning, and dressing them as Brad had always done.

"On the third night, after Brad slipped into coma, his heart finally stopped at about 3 A.M. Everyone in the cabin awoke. We made tea and talked quietly. Then Donna, another friend, and I bathed his body, rubbed him in lanolin, and dressed him in wool. He was the best-dressed person there! We wrapped him in four sheep skins and placed him on a bier that several of the men had made from maple saplings lashed together with pea netting stretched across the frame for support. We carried him down past the vegetable garden, to a clearing at the edge of the woods where a grave had been dug just where he had wanted it. We lined the grave with pine boughs, then lowered Brad into it. There were fourteen of us. We shoveled dirt on top of him until the grave was filled. Then we prayed, sang songs, and cried a lot. After lunch we went back and finished up with the lambs. It was such a dignified death: There were no strangers involved."

Many cultures bury their dead directly in the earth so that nothing will interfere with the disintegration of the physical body. In some Christian churches on Ash Wednesday, the first day of Lent, a forty-day period of fasting and penitence prior to Easter, people come to have ashes placed on their foreheads. As the priest makes the sign of the cross in ashes, he or she repeats, "Remember, oh man, from dust thou art and to dust thou shalt return."

The Court of Heaven

Hasidic Jewish: Ukraine

This story is about Reb Noah. He was a student of Lubavitch. He died and came to the Court of Heaven. They looked into his case and they found out that all his life he had observed everything that he should in the highest way. Angels came who were born from his good deeds and they were witnesses for him: "I was born from this good deed." Thousands of angels came who had been born from the good deeds of this holy man. And the Court was going to decide that he should go immediately to Paradise.

All of a sudden an angel appeared and he said, "Wait a second! I have to tell something about him." And he said, "I was created from one bad deed that this holy man did in his lifetime." And he brought out what he did.

The Court of Heaven deliberated and they said he should have either one half hour in Gehenna [Hell] or he should be reborn on earth to fix what he had failed to do the first time. Reb Noah answered the court that all his life everything that he had to decide he asked his Rebbe. He never did anything without asking the Rebbe; therefore he wanted to ask his trusted Rebbe to tell now what he should decide. They looked over his records in the Court of Heaven and they found out that he was right. Everything he did he had asked his Rebbe's permission.

From *Legends of the Hasidim: An Introduction to Hasidic Tradition and Oral culture in the New World*, by Jerome Mintz, pp.251–252 (Chicago: University of Chicago Press, 1968). Used with permission.

The Rebbe, Rabbi Shneur Zalman, was sitting with his *hasidim* and he said to them, "Reb Noah is asking now what he should select: either Gehenna, a half hour of hell, or be reborn in the world a second time." They had nothing to say. They were waiting. And the Rebbe put his holy hand on his forehead and he rested his head on the table for a short time. Then he said: "Gehenna . . . Gehenna." In the second when the Rebbe said the word Gehenna, they heard a voice, "Oy, Rebbe!" And they saw on the wall by the door, the mark of a burned hand — the fingers of a hand burned into the wall.

This story is adapted from a Hasidic folktale. The Hasidic movement, a charismatic form of Judaism, started in the middle of the eighteenth century in the Ukraine and spread rapidly throughout Eastern Europe.

The tale of the holy man, Noah, is unusual in that it introduces the possibility of choice in the afterlife. Noah has to decide how he is going to make retribution for his misdeed. There is no question of getting off the hook; either he comes back for another lifetime and pays for his wrong doing or is punished by a brief measure of torment. In this way we are reminded that we all have that same choice during our lives, once we are aware of having committed a misdeed. We cannot change the past, but we can make amends for our mistakes by confronting the truth and adjusting our behavior. Or we can do nothing and live with our guilt, which carries its own form of excruciating self-torment.

There is an unfinished, mysterious quality to this story that mirrors many lives. What is the meaning of the burned hand on the wall? Is it a warning to those still living of the consequences of bad deeds? Is it Noah's gift or his revenge? As in the ancient cave paintings and pictographs found around the world, we can only speculate on the meaning.

Life and Death

African: The Hausa of western Africa

There were two old men who journeyed together. The name of one was Life, and the other was called Death. They came to a place where a spring flowed, and the man who owned the spring greeted them. They asked him for permission to drink. He said, "Yes, drink. But let the elder drink first, because that is the custom."

Life said, "I, indeed am the elder."

Death said, "No, I am the elder."

Life answered, "How can that be? Life came first. Without living things to die, Death does not exist."

Death said, "On the contrary, before Life was born everything was Death. Living things come out of Death, go on a while, and then return to Death."

Life replied, "Surely that is not the way it is. Before Life, there was no Death, merely that which is not seen. The Creator made this world out of the unseen substances. When the first person died, that was the beginning of Death. Therefore you, Death, are the younger."

Death argued, "Death is merely what we do not know. When the Creator created, he molded everything out of what we do not know. Therefore Death is like a father to Life."

They disputed this way standing beside the spring. And at last they asked the owner of the water to judge the dispute. He said, "How can one speak of Death without Life, from which it proceeds? And how can one speak of Life without Death, to which all living things go? Both of you have spoken eloquently. Your words are true. Neither can exist without the other. Neither of you is senior. Neither of you is junior. Life and Death are merely two faces [masks] of the Creator. Therefore you are of equal age. Here is a gourd of water. Drink from it together."

They received the gourd of water. They drank. And after that they continued their journey. What say you to these travelers? They go from one place to another in each other's company. Can one be the elder and the other the younger? If you do not know, let us consider other things.

The argument in this story is not about whether there should be life or death, as in the Native American folktale "The Argument," but rather which is more important and therefore more powerful. The wisdom, one might say the punch line, is found appropriately in the very end: "If you do not know, let us consider other things."

LESSONS FOR LIFE

Parting is all we know of heaven, and all we need of hell.

EMILY DICKINSON

The stories in this section, while they all touch on death in one way or another, are really about life. They suggest that what we do, how we relate to one another, has consequences. In an odd way I think they speak to the ego, the self that asks, "But why me? What have I done to deserve this?"or, as in "The Death of Great Sun," the self that declares, "I will control both life and death!" Each story has a different focus and is in no way to be compared to another. Rather they are grouped together to show a diversity of lessons for life.

The Cow-Tail Switch

African: The Jabo of Liberia

Near the edge of the Liberian rain forest, on a hill overlooking the Cavally River, was the village of Kundi. Its rice and cassava fields spread in all directions. Cattle grazed in the grassland near the river. Smoke from fires in the round clay houses seeped through the palm-leaf roofs, and from a distance these faint columns of smoke seemed to hover over the village. Men and boys fished in the river with nets, and women pounded grain in wooden mortars before the houses.

In this village, with his wife and many children, lived a hunter by the name of Ogaloussa. One morning Ogaloussa took his weapons down from the wall of his house and went into the forest to hunt. His wife and his children went to tend their fields and drove their cattle out to graze. The day passed, and they ate their evening meal of manioc and fish. Darkness came, but Ogaloussa didn't return.

Another day went by and still Ogaloussa didn't come back. They talked about it and wondered what could have detained him. A week passed, then a month. Sometimes Ogaloussa's sons mentioned that he hadn't come home. The family cared for the crops, and the sons hunted for game, but after a while they no longer talked about Ogaloussa's disappearance.

From *The Cow-Tail Switch and Other West African Stories,* by Harold Courlander, copyright 1947, 1975 by Harold Courlander. Reprinted by permission of Henry Holt & Company, Inc.

Then, one day, another son was born to Ogaloussa's wife. His name was Puli. Puli grew older. He began to sit up and crawl. The time came when Puli began to talk, and the first thing he said was, "Where is my father?"

The other sons looked across the ricefields.

"Yes," one of them said. "Where is father?"

"He should have returned long ago," another one said.

"Something must have happened. We ought to look for him," a third son said.

"He went into the forest, but where will we find him?" another one asked.

"I saw him go," one of them said. "He went that way, across the river. Let us follow the trail and search for him."

So the sons took their weapons and started out to look for Ogaloussa. When they were deep among the great trees and vines of the forest they lost their trail. They searched in the forest until one of them found the trail again. They followed it until they lost the way once more, and then another son found the trail. It was dark in the forest and many times they became lost. Each time another son found the way. At last they came to a clearing among the trees, and there scattered about on the ground lay Ogaloussa's bones and his rusted weapons. They knew then that Ogaloussa had been killed in the hunt.

One of the sons stepped forward and said, "I know how to put a dead person's bones together." He gathered all of Ogaloussa's bones and put them together, each in its right place.

Another son said, "I have knowledge too. I know how to cover the skeleton with sinews and flesh." He went to work and covered Ogaloussa's bones with sinews and flesh.

A third son said, "I have the power to put blood into the body." He went forward and put blood into Ogaloussa's veins, and then he stepped aside.

Another son said, "I can put breath into a body." He did his work, and when he was through they saw Ogaloussa's chest rise and fall.

"I can give the power of movement to a body," another of them said. He put the power of movement into his father's body, and Ogaloussa sat up and opened his eyes.

"I can give him the power of speech," another son said. He gave the body the power of speech, and then he stepped back.

Ogaloussa looked around him. He stood up. "Where are my weapons?" he asked.

They picked up his rusted weapons from the grass where they lay and gave them to him. Then they returned the way they had come, through the forest and the rice-fields, until they had arrived once more in the village.

Ogaloussa went into his house. His wife prepared a bath for him and he bathed. She prepared food for him and he ate. Four days he remained in the house, and on the fifth day he came out and shaved his head, because this was what people did when they came back from the land of the dead.

Afterwards, he killed a cow for a great feast. He took the cow's tail and braided it. He decorated it with beads and cowry shells and bits of shiny metal. It was a beautiful thing. Ogaloussa carried it with him to important affairs. When there was a dance or important ceremony he always had it with him. The people of the village thought it was the most beautiful cow-tail switch they had ever seen.

Soon there was a celebration in the village because Ogaloussa had returned from the dead. The people dressed in their best clothes, the musicians brought out their instruments, and a big dance began. The drummers beat their drums and the women sang. The people drank much palm wine. Everyone was happy.

Ogaloussa carried his cow-tail switch and everyone admired it. Some of the men grew bold and came forward to Ogaloussa and asked for the cow-tail switch, but Ogaloussa kept it in his hand. Now and then there was a clamor and much confusion as many people asked for it at once. The women and children begged for it too, but Ogaloussa refused them all.

Finally he stood up to talk. The dancing stopped and people came close to hear what Ogaloussa had to say.

"A long time ago I went into the forest," Ogaloussa said. "While I was hunting I was killed by a leopard. Then my sons came for me. They brought me back from the land of the dead to my village. I will give this cow-tail switch to one of my sons. All of them have done something to bring me back from the dead, but I have only one cow tail to give. I shall give it to the one who did the most to bring me home."

So an argument started.

"He will give it to me!" one of the sons said. "It was I who did the most, for I found the trail in the forest when it was lost!"

"No, he will give it to me!" another son said. "It was I who put his bones together!"

"It was I who covered his bones with sinews and flesh!" another said. "He will give it to me!"

"It was I who gave him the power of movement!" another son said. "I deserve it most!"

Another son said it was he who should have the switch, because he had put blood in Ogaloussa's veins. Another claimed it because he had put breath in the body. Each of the sons argued his right to possess the wonderful cow-tail switch.

Before long not only the sons but the other people of the village were talking. Some of them argued that the son who had put blood in Ogaloussa's vein should get the switch, others that the one who had given Ogaloussa's breath should get it. Some of them believed that all of the sons had done equal things, and that they should share it. They argued back and forth this way until Ogaloussa asked them to be quiet.

"To this son I will give the cow-tail switch, for I owe most to him," Ogaloussa said.

He came forward and bent low and handed it to Puli, the little boy who had been born while Ogaloussa was in the forest.

The people of the village remembered then that the child's first words had been, "Where is my father?" They knew that Ogaloussa was right.

For it was a saying among them that a man is not really dead until he is forgotten.

The message that this story carries can have interesting connotations for us today, living as we do in a society where every day highly trained doctors and others intercede with complex technology to bring people back from the brink of death. In "The Cow-Tail Switch," the miracles performed by the various sons to revive their father, important as they were to Ogaloussa's return to his people, were less powerful than little Puli's question "Where is my father?" To remember, the story tells us, is the most powerful tool we have to keep our loved ones "alive."

*They felt strange chills as though they were beginning to change
into the forms of hidden water creatures.*

The Swirling Red River

Native American: The Zuni of New Mexico

Once, long ago, a group of families called a clan, were traveling when they came to the banks of a great river, whose red waters swirled and churned before them. The people were afraid to cross such a formidable stream. The fathers of the clan gathered in a circle to deliberate amongst themselves and then abruptly strode into the red waters, feeling with their feet for footing as they led the way across. Their fearlessness was great, for as they inched forward, the waters moved beneath them and they felt strange chills as though they were beginning to change into the forms of hidden water creatures. Nevertheless they won their way to the opposite shore.

The women with their children on their backs were the next to venture into the river. They were more susceptible to the aura of these strange waters and became panic-stricken and witless with fear. The children, being as yet unfinished and immature, changed instantly in their terror. Their skins turned cold and scaly, and they grew tails. Their hands and feet became webbed and clawed as if suitable for swimming in those disquieting waters. To their mothers the children felt like dead things that scratched and clung on their bare shoulders. Shrieking wildly, the mothers cast their children away and fled to the far shore in terror.

Adapted from "The Abode of Souls," in *The Mythic World of the Zuni,* by Frank Hamilton Cushing, edited and illustrated by Barton Wright, pp. 58–59 (Albuquerque: The University of New Mexico Press, 1988).

Wailing piteously, many of the children fell into the swift waters. Their shrill and plaintive calls could be heard even from under the water — as it is said they may still be heard at night near lonely waters.

No sooner did the children sink beneath the waters than they changed even more. Some became lizards, others frogs, turtles, or newts. But their souls sank through the waters of the lagoon below the hollow mountain into the abode of ghosts, where the finished souls of ancient men of war and violent death resided. In this place there was a pueblo called the Town of Towns with a great six-chambered assembly house of the spirits. Here sat the god priests in council. It was here, also, that the priests taught to the newly dead the Dance of Good and received from them the messages and offerings of mortal men.

Now, when the little children sank into the dark depths, the lights of the spirit dancers began to break upon them, and they became as the ancients. Having been received by these undying souls, they thus took the pathway that all souls must follow. But the mothers, not knowing their children had returned unharmed to the spirit world, where in time they too would go, loudly wailed on the far shore of the river.

As the people wailed and mourned their lost children, suddenly they heard a comforting voice speak to them. "Cease your clamor, good people, let go of your terror! Your children are safe in the assembly house of the spirits with the ancients to comfort them. Let this be a lesson to you; cherish your children through all dangers and behave not like birds, abandoning your offspring at the first threat. For," the voice continued, "the magic of the waters will pass when you emerge from them and all will be as before!" Thus those who had yet to pass through the river took heart and, clutching their children to them, they won their way through the swirling red waters to the opposite shore.

This story comes to us from the Zuni tribe in the American Southwest. More than one anthropologist has commented on the unusual belief system of the Zunis, which differs in many respects from those of other Native Americans. According to Dennis Tedlock, [the Zunis believe that] "accidental deaths are the result of not being in right relationship with the cosmos."[†] This story is an example of that belief, spelled out by the mysterious "voice," which admonishes the women, "Behave not like birds, abandoning your offspring at the first threat."

Notice that the anguished women seem unaware of the spiritual fate of their lost children's souls, so distracted are they by the horrors of the immediate catastrophe. How often our religious upbringing or spiritual beliefs seem meaningless when we are unexpectedly faced with the death of a loved one, especially when that loved one is a child. And when there is any suggestion of parental responsibility in the death, the anguish is indeed intense.

In some cultures, the death of a young person is treated very differently from that of one who has lived a full life. In West Africa, for instance, "Mourning for the young is in private, by near kin only. Early death so offends that it is hidden from society at large." By contrast, "When the very old die, there are displays of joy — often on a grand scale."[†]

[†] Morton-Williams, Peter, "Yoruba Responses to the Fear of Death," *Africa: Journal of the International Institute,* edited by Daryll Forde, vol.30, pp.34–40 (London: Oxford University Press, 1960).

The Messengers of Death

German: Grimm Brothers

In olden times a giant was once traveling along the great highway. Then a stranger suddenly jumped at him, crying, "Halt! Not a step farther!"

"What!" said the giant, "you little creature that I can squeeze to death between my fingers, do you mean to block my way? Who are you to speak so boldly?"

"I am Death," replied the other. "No one opposes me, and even you must obey my command." But the giant rebelled and started to wrestle with Death. It was a long hard struggle; finally the giant gained the upper hand and struck Death down with his fist so that he collapsed by a stone. The giant went his way and Death lay there conquered and was so impotent that he couldn't get up again. "What is to happen," he said, "if I lie here in the corner? No one will die in the world any more, and it will get so full of people that they will no longer have any room to stand beside one another."

As he was saying this, a young man came along, vigorous and healthy, singing a song and glancing here and there. When he spied the half-unconscious man, he went sympathetically to him, lifted him up, gave him a fortifying drink from his bottle, and waited until the latter had regained his strength. Raising himself, the stranger asked, "But do you know who I am, and whom you have helped to his feet again?"

"The Messengers of Death," in *The Grimms German Folk Tales,* translated by Francis P.Magoun Jr. and Alexander H. Krappe, pp. 570–571 (Carbondale: Southern Illinois University Press, 1960). Copyright ©1960 by Southern Illinois Press. Used with permission.

"No," answered the youth, "I don't know you."

"I am Death," he said; "I spare no one nor can I make an exception in your case. But that you may see that I am grateful, I promise not to assail you unawares but shall first send my messengers before I come to fetch you."

"All right," said the youth. "It's at least something to know when you're coming and to be safe from you that long." Then he went on, was merry and in good spirits, and lived a happy-go-lucky life.

But youth and health did not last long. Soon came illnesses and pains that tormented him by day and gave him no rest by night. "I shan't die," he said to himself, "for Death will first send his messengers; I only wish that the evil days of illness were over." As soon as he felt well, he began again to live merrily.

Then one day someone tapped him on the shoulder. He looked around and Death was standing behind him and said, "Follow me! Your hour of departure from the World has come."

"What! are you going to break your word?" answered the man. "Didn't you promise to send your messengers to me before you yourself came? I haven't seen any."

"Quiet!" replied Death. "Didn't I send you one messenger after another? Didn't Fever come, attack you, shake you and overthrow you? Didn't Giddiness stupefy your brain? Didn't Gout give you twinges in every limb? Didn't your ears buzz? Didn't Toothache wrack your jaws? Didn't it go black before your eyes? Over and above all that, didn't Sleep, my own brother, remind you of me every night? Didn't you lie at night as if you were already dead?" The man had no answer, yielded to his fate, and went away with Death.

This story has many popular versions today; one hears them from pulpits and lecterns in a variety of contexts. Sometimes God sends the messengers of death rather than Death himself. Regardless of the particulars, however, the lesson is clear. We need to pay attention to the events of our lives: They are messages sent to give us guidance, if we but heed them. Not only does no one escape death, but change in all its many guises is inevitable. The more awake and aware we are of the signs and signals along the way, the better prepared and more accepting we can be to handle transitions. How many times have we heard, "My husband (wife) walked out on me one day with no warning." Or "They just fired me for no reason." Those people weren't picking up their messages.

In this tale collected by the Grimm brothers, an added element is introduced that shines a different light on death. Here Death is all but vanquished by the giant. Who is this powerful giant that he is able to overthrow Death? Today we might say that he symbolizes our enormous faith in science and technology or our powerful belief in materialism. In any event, Death is left helpless and unable to move until the young man comes along and takes pity on him. At this point in the story, we are reminded of the parable of the Good Samaritan: An unlikely character comes to the rescue. In the end, the happy-go-lucky man becomes Everyman, and Death resumes his familiar role.

Death of Great Sun

Native American: The Natchez of the Midwest

The Great Sun lies cold and pale upon his bed. His servants bring food and his wife offers it to the dead man. "Do you not wish to enjoy the food we bring to you?" she asks. "You make no answer. Therefore you must surely be dead, and have left us to go to the land of the spirits!"

Now the wife weeps in agony, throwing back her head and howling her death cry. The sound is taken up by all the attendants and relatives of the great ruler. The cry echoes from house to house until the entire village resounds with the lamentation.

For two days elaborate preparations for the funeral are undertaken by the people. The Great Sun lies in state, adorned in his finest regalia, his face painted red. By his side are the emblems of his power: a war club, numerous stone pipes handsomely carved to commemorate his victories, his bow and arrow, and a chain of cane woven with a succession of links, each representing an enemy he killed in battle. Surrounding his bed are his retainers and his wife, silently awaiting the gruesome rite which is their customary role in the burial of a great person.

Now whispers arise as the High Priest makes his splendid entrance, elaborately tattooed and dressed in feathers and shell beads. At a signal from the priest, the attendants lift the litter of the dead king. Now the solemn procession begins. It winds down the stately mound on which the Great Sun's house is perched, slowly

From Native Land *by Jamake Highwater, ©1997; original edition: Little Brown & Co.; reprint: Baker & Taylor; excerpted with the permission of The Native Land Foundation.*

making its way into the plaza. The ruler is carried in a wide circle among the silent people who fill the plaza and each of the dead man's retainers is joined by eight relatives, their arms and hands painted red. Eventually, these relatives will be the executioners of their own kin — a ritual that is central to the funeral of the Great Sun.

Now the litter bearing the dead man is carried toward the temple mound that flanks the plaza. A group of women raise their voices in the doleful chant of death, as the procession starts the climb to the temple. Suddenly there is a great outcry and the strangled corpses of infants are cast under the feet of the litter bearers. The children are sacrifices, killed by their own parents, whose social rank is increased by their terrible offering to the dead king.

The cortege ascends to the summit of the truncated mound, where the retainers and the wife of the Great Sun dutifully take their places on mats which have been spread on each side of the dead man's litter. Now the funeral ceremony begins. The High Priest asks the Great Sun's wife: "Is it your wish to live forever with your great husband and to go with him to the land of the spirits?"

"Yes!" she exclaims, "for in that land we have never to die again. The days are beautiful and there is abundant food, and people are peaceful and do not make war upon one another for they are all of one family!"

The priest then asks the same question of the fifty retainers, and they cry: "Yes! We wish to accompany our king to the land of the spirits!"

The death chant rises abruptly and a dance begins, figures weaving in and out among the sacrificial victims, who sit upon the mats and move solemnly to the rhythm of the singing.

As the music swells and the voices rise to a shrill pitch, each victim is given a ball of narcotic herbs, which is quickly swallowed. Soon they become drowsy and begin to slip into unconsciousness. They smile peacefully as a cord is placed around their necks and relatives assemble beside each victim, four on each side, grasping the cord tightly in their hands.

The High Priest stands before the eternal flame that burns in the temple. He lifts his ceremonial staff and brings it to the earth with an elegant gesture. The cords are drawn tight, and the fifty retainers struggle momentarily and then slump to the ground. The dead king is now surrounded by a large ensemble of corpses who will accompany him into the land of the spirits.

The howls rise louder than ever, and to the accompaniment of this immense lamentation the bodies are carried to the summit of the burial mound and placed in graves along with offerings of fine ornaments, weapons, and pottery. Slowly the graves are filled, while on the mound across the village where the Great Sun once lived a cloud of smoke rises as the royal house is burned to the ground.

This story, unlike the others in the collection, is the retelling of an eyewitness account by the Jesuit missionary Father le Petit. In a letter written in 1730, he describes the mortuary rites of a group (now extinct) of Midwestern Native American Mound Builders known as the Natchez. While it may be difficult for present-day readers to understand and assimilate the facts of this event, it is included here because it addresses the troubling question of mass sacrificial death. In 1996 the world looked on in horror, presumably much as Father le Petit did, to the unfolding events at Waco, Texas, and fifteen years before that at Jonesville, Guyana. Because most of us have no way to accept such events, we resort to angry blame and recrimination. The fact is that individual and group human sacrifice has been practiced in various forms throughout history. Sending people off to die in war is a form of human sacrifice still condoned by a large portion of humanity. We honor our war dead through ceremony and build monuments to their sacrifice for their country. Today the nations of the world who have declared their unwillingness to participate in human sacrifice through warfare can be counted on the fingers of one hand.

All those, save the babies, involved in the Natchez death ritual participated willingly and, if one is to believe Father le Petit's account, eagerly. They believed they would be rewarded in the afterlife by their ultimate sacrifice. The parents of the slain babies would win their promotions even sooner. Unlike the many groups of religious ascetics throughout history who practice self-denial and self-punishment in this life in the hopes of a better life in the hereafter, the Natchez denied themselves nothing. The opportunity to give their lives for their sun king was their supreme reward.

Heaven and Hell

Origin Unknown

There was a man who wanted to know what heaven and hell were really like. He prayed and prayed, and finally he was allowed to visit and see for himself. First he was sent to hell. When he got there, he saw a long banquet table laden with the most delicious food imaginable. There were great baskets of fresh-baked breads, hundreds of cheeses from around the world, platters of succulent meats, fresh vegetables of every variety, lightly tossed salads of tender greens from the garden. There were bowls brimming with ripe fruit and berries, steaming puddings and glistening pies emitting tantalizing aromas, as well as all manner of other elegant desserts, cookies, and candy confections. Never before had he seen such a splendid array; the table seemed to stretch on forever. Yet along each side of the banquet table he saw a multitude of people weeping and moaning in distress. What could be the meaning of this outcry, he wondered? Then he noticed that no one was eating any of the food. He drew closer and saw that to the front and back of each person's arms were strapped boards so that they were unable to bend their elbows. No matter how they contorted themselves, they could not get the food into their mouths. Now he understood the cause of their misery.

Then the man was shown into heaven. To his surprise, he found the same banquet table laden with the same splendid array. There were the baskets of fresh breads, the hundreds of cheeses from around the world, the platters of succulent meats, the fresh vegetables and garden greens, the bowls brimming with ripe fruit and berries, the steaming puddings and glistening pies, the other elegant desserts, cookies, and candy confections. Once again, on each side of the table throngs of people were gathered. And here, too, they had boards strapped to the front and backs of their elbows. But unlike the scene in hell, here no one was weeping or wailing. As he gazed down the long banquet table, the man saw smiling faces and heard only cries of delight. For here the people had solved the dilemma of not being able to reach their mouths to eat. They were happily feeding one another. "Ah," said the man, "Now I understand the difference between heaven and hell."

The first time I encountered this story in 1980, a storyteller friend told it in a workshop. In her version, the people had no elbows. When I inquired recently as to its source, she said that she had heard it from another storyteller. Since then I have heard several versions, including one told by Stephen Levine. The only written version I have uncovered is a Chinese one that has the people struggling with impossibly long chopsticks. Clearly this tale has traveled around the world from who knows what source and been adapted by different storytellers along the way. I see this as a splendid example of the bardic tradition at work in the world. The real wealth of any culture is the wisdom that is passed on from generation to generation. It is only valuable when it is held in people's conscious awareness.

In its essence, the message here relates to the New Testament story of the loaves and fishes. It reminds us that as people begin to share what they have, they can glimpse unsuspected abundance. Heaven and hell, the story intimates, are not so much about far distant places but rather about internal states of awareness and current patterns of action. People in luxurious circumstances can be miserable, just as people in adversity can experience fulfillment and even joy.

Thus, the story suggests that we can know both heaven and hell in this life as well as after death, depending on our choices.

The Death-Stone

Buddhist: Japan

The Death-Stone stands on Nasu's moor
Through winter snows and summer heat;
The moss grows grey upon its sides,
But the foul demon haunts it yet.

Chill blows the blast: the owl's sad choir
Hoots hoarsely through the moaning pines;
Among the low chrysanthemums.
The skulking fox, the jackal whines,
As o'er the moor the autumn light declines.

The Buddhist priest Genno, after much weary travel, came to the moor of Nasu, and was about to rest under the shadow of a great stone, when a spirit suddenly appeared and said: "Rest not under this stone. This is the Death-Stone. Men, birds, and beasts have perished by merely touching it!"

These mysterious and warning remarks naturally awakened Genno's curiosity, and he begged that the spirit would favor him with the story of the Death-Stone.

Thus the spirit began: "Long ago there was a fair girl living at the Japanese Court. She was so charming that she was called the Jewel Maiden. Her wisdom equalled her beauty, for she understood Buddhist lore and the Confucian classics, science, and the poetry of China."

"The Death-Stone," in *Myths and Legends of Japan,* by F. Hadland Davis, pp. 95–98 (London: George G. Harrap & Co., 1912). Legend quotations translated by B. H. Chamberlain. Reprinted with permission.

So sweetly decked by nature and by art,
The monarch's self soon clasp'd her to his heart.

"One night," went on the spirit, "the Mikado gave a great feast in the Summer Palace, and there he assembled the wit, wisdom, and beauty of the land. It was a brilliant gathering; but while the company ate and drank, accompanied by the strains of sweet music, darkness crept over the great apartment. Black clouds raced across the sky, and there was not a star to be seen. While the guests sat rigid with fear a mysterious wind arose. It howled throughout the Summer Palace and blew out all the lanterns. The complete darkness produced a state of panic, and during the uproar someone cried out, 'A light! A light!'"

And lo! from out the Jewel Maiden's frame
There's seen to dart a weirdly lustrous flame!
It grows, it spreads, it fills th' imperial halls;
The painted screens, the costly panell'd walls,
Erst the pale viewless damask of the night
Sparkling stand forth as in the moon's full light.

"From that very hour the Mikado sickened," continued the spirit. "He grew so ill that the Court Magician was sent for, and this worthy soul speedily ascertained the cause of his majesty's decline. He stated, with much warmth of language, that the Jewel Maiden was a harlot and a fiend, 'who, with insidious art, the State to ravage, captivates thy heart!'

"The Magician's words turned the Mikado's heart against the Jewel Maiden. When this sorceress was spurned she resumed her original shape, that of a fox, and ran away to this very stone on Nasu moor."

The priest looked at the spirit critically. "Who are you?" he said at length.

"I am the demon that once dwelt in the breast of the Jewel Maiden!
Now I inhabit the Death-Stone for evermore!"

"I am the demon that once dwelt in the breast of the Jewel Maiden! Now I inhabit the Death-Stone for evermore!"

The good Genno was much horrified by this dreadful confession, but remembering his duty as a priest, he said: "Though you have sunk low in wickedness, you shall rise to virtue again. Take this priestly robe and begging-bowl, and reveal to me your fox form."

Then this wicked spirit cried pitifully:
In the garish light of day
I hide myself away,
Like pale Asama's fires:
With the night I'll come again,
Confess my guilt with pain
And new-born pure desires.

With these words the spirit suddenly vanished.

Genno did not relinquish his good intentions. He strove more ardently than ever for this erring soul's salvation. In order that she might attain Nirvana, he offered flowers, burnt incense, and recited the sacred Scriptures in front of the stone.

When Genno had performed these religious duties, he said: "Spirit of the Death-Stone, I conjure thee! What was it in a former world that did cause thee to assume in this so foul a shape?"

Suddenly the Death-Stone was rent and the spirit once more appeared, crying:

In stones there are spirits,
In the waters is a voice heard:
The winds sweep across the firmament!

Genno saw a lurid glare about him and, in the shining light, a fox that suddenly turned into a beautiful maiden.

Thus spoke the spirit of the Death-Stone: "I am she who first, in Ind, was the demon to whom Prince Hazoku paid homage . . . . In Great Cathay I took the form of Hoji, consort of the Emperor Iuwao; and at the court of the Rising Sun I became the flawless Jewel Maiden, concubine to the Emperor Toba."

The spirit confessed to Genno that in the form of the Jewel Maiden she had desired to bring destruction to the Imperial line. "Already," said the spirit, "I was making my plans, already I was gloating over the thought of the Mikado's death, and had it not been for the power of the Court Magician I should have succeeded in my scheme. As I have told you, I was driven from the Court. I was pursued by dogs and arrows, and finally sank exhausted into the Death-Stone. From time to time I haunt the moor. Now the Lord Buddha has had compassion upon me, and he has sent his priest to point out the way of true religion and to bring peace."

The legend concludes with the following pious utterances poured forth by the now contrite spirit:

> "I swear, O man of God! I swear," she cries,
> "To thee whose blessing wafts me to the skies,
> I swear a solemn oath, that shall endure
> Firm as the Death-Stone standing on the moor,
> That from this hour I'm virtue's child alone!"
> Thus spake the ghoul, and vanished 'neath the Stone.

Here we have several different themes interacting. There is the idea of evil being able to inhabit and affect not just people but other creatures and inanimate objects as well. In this story, evil functions as a separate and discrete force, strong-willed and powerful. The soul is capable of redemption but only when evil is driven out. Then there is the belief that the soul has many lives and is reincarnated in various personalities but retains an inner identity. Transformation is another related theme. The spirit in the Death-Stone is able to transform itself at will from one form to another: spirit, fox, Jewel Maiden, ghoul. Finally there is the theme, ever present in Buddhist lore, of compassion. The priest Genno is not willing to abandon the spirit, realizing its tortured existence, and so labors mightily to exorcise the evil force and bring the cleansed soul to Nirvana, a place of great peace.

The Death of Baldur

Norse: Scandinavia

Baldur, the god of light, peace, virtue, and wisdom, having been tormented with terrible dreams indicating that his life was in peril, told them to the assembled gods, who resolved to conjure all things to avert from him the threatened danger. Then Frigga, the mother of Baldur, wife of Odin, and goddess of the skies and the home, exacted an oath from fire and water, from iron and all other metals, from stones, trees, diseases, beasts, birds, poisons, and creeping things, that none of them would do any harm to Baldur. Odin, chief deity and god of art, culture, war, and the dead, not satisfied with this, and feeling alarmed for the fate of his son, determined to consult the prophetess Angerbode, a giantess, mother of Hela, who presided over the land of the dead known as Hel. Now Angerbode was herself dead so Odin was forced to seek her in Hela's domain.

But meanwhile, the other gods, feeling that what Frigga had done was quite sufficient, amused themselves with using Baldur as a mark, some hurling darts at him, some stones, while others hewed at him with their swords and battle-axes; for do what they would, none of them could harm him. And this became a favorite pastime with them and was regarded as an honor shown to Baldur. But when Loki, who never ceased to work evil among gods and men, beheld the scene, he was sorely vexed that Baldur was not hurt. Assuming, therefore, the shape of a woman, he went

"The Death of Baldur," in *Mythology: The Age of Fable, The Age of Chivalry, Legends of Charlemagne,* by Thomas Bulfinch, pp. 343–347 (New York: Thomas Y. Crowell Co., 1913).

to Fensalir, the mansion of Frigga. That goddess, when she saw the pretended woman, inquired of her if she knew what the gods were doing at their meetings. She replied that they were throwing darts and stones at Baldur, without being able to hurt him. "Ay," said Frigga, "neither stones, nor sticks, nor anything else can hurt Baldur, for I have exacted an oath from all of them."

"What," exclaimed the woman, "have all things sworn to spare Baldur?"

"All things," replied Frigga, "except one little shrub that grows on the eastern side of Odin's great hall, Valhalla, and is called Mistletoe, and which I thought too young and feeble to crave an oath from."

As soon as Loki heard this he went away and resuming his natural shape, cut off the mistletoe, and repaired to the place where the gods were assembled. There he found Hodur standing apart, without partaking of the sports, on account of his blindness, and going up to him, said, "Why dost thou not throw something at Baldur?"

"Because I am blind," answered Hodur, "and see not where Baldur is, and have, moreover, nothing to throw."

"Come, then," said Loki, "do like the rest, and show honor to Baldur by throwing this twig at him, and I will direct thy arm towards the place where he stands."

Hodur then took the mistletoe, and under the guidance of Loki, darted it at Baldur, who, pierced through and through, fell down lifeless. Surely never was there witnessed, either among gods or men, a more atrocious deed than this. When Baldur fell, the gods were struck speechless with horror, and then they looked at each other, and all were of one mind to lay hands on him who had done the deed, but they were obliged to delay their vengeance out of respect for the sacred place where they were assembled. They gave vent to their grief by loud lamentations. When the gods came to themselves, Frigga asked who among them wished to gain all her love and good will. "For this shall he have," said she, "who will ride to Hel and offer Hela a ransom if she will let Baldur return here to Asgard, our home." Whereupon Hermod, surnamed the Nimble, another son of Odin, offered to undertake the journey. Odin's horse, Sleipnir, which has eight legs and can outrun the wind, was then led forth, on which Hermod mounted and galloped away on his mission. For the space of nine days and as many nights he rode through deep glens so dark they he could not discern anything, until he arrived at the river Gyoll, which he passed over on a bridge covered with glittering gold. The maiden who kept the bridge asked him his name and lineage, telling him that the day before five bands of dead persons had ridden over the bridge, and did not shake it as much as he alone. "But," she added, "thou hast not death's hue on thee; why then ridest thou here on the way to Hel?"

"I ride to Hel," answered Hermod, "to seek Baldur. Hast thou perchance seen him pass this way?"

She replied, "Baldur hath ridden over Gyoll's bridge, and yonder lieth the way he took to the abodes of death."

Hermod pursued his journey until he came to the barred gates of Hel. Here he alighted, girthed his saddle tighter, and remounting clapped both spurs to his horse, who cleared the gate by a tremendous leap without touching it. Hermod then rode on to the palace, where he found his brother Baldur occupying the most distinguished seat in the hall, and passed the night in his company. The next morning he besought Hela to let Baldur ride home with him, assuring her that nothing but lamentations were to be heard among the gods. Hela answered that it should now be tried whether Baldur was so beloved as he was said to be. "If, therefore," she added, "all things in the world, both living and lifeless, weep for him, then shall he return to life; but if any one thing speak against him or refuse to weep, he shall be kept in Hel."

Hermod then rode back to Asgard and gave an account of all he had heard and witnessed.

The gods upon this news dispatched messengers throughout the world to beg everything to weep in order that Baldur might be delivered from Hel. All things very willingly complied with this request, both men and every other living being, as well as earths, and stones, and trees, and metals, just as we have all seen these things weep when they are brought from a cold place into a hot one. As the messengers were returning, they found an old hag named Thaukt sitting in a cavern, and begged her to weep Baldur out of Hel. But she answered,

> "Thaukt will wail
> With dry tears
> Baldur's bale-fire.
> Let Hela keep her own."

It was strongly suspected that this hag was no other than Loki himself, on his never ending mission to work evil. So Baldur was prevented from coming back to Asgard and to life.

Then the gods took up the dead body and bore it to the seashore where stood Baldur's ship, "Hringham," which passed for the largest in the world. Baldur's dead body was put on the funeral pile, on board the ship, and his wife, Nanna, was so struck with grief at the sight that she broke her heart, and her body was burned on the same pile as her husband's. There was a vast concourse of various kinds of people at Baldur's funeral. First came Odin accompanied by Frigga, the maidens who accompany and attend fallen heros to Valhalla: the Valkyrie, and his ravens; then

Frey, the god of crops, fruitfulness, love, peace, and prosperity, in his cart drawn by Gullinbursti, the boar; Heimdall, the watchman of Asgard, rode his horse, Gulltopp, and Freya, sister of Frey and goddess of love and beauty, drove in her chariot drawn by cats. There were also a great many Frost giants and giants of the mountains present. Baldur's horse was led to the pile fully adorned and consumed in the same flames with his master.

But Loki did not escape his deserved punishment. When he saw how angry the gods were, he fled to the mountain, and there built himself a hut with four doors, so that he could see every approaching danger. He invented a net to catch the fishes, such as fishermen have used since his time. But Odin found out his hiding place and the gods assembled to take him. He, seeing this, changed himself into a salmon, and lay hid among the stones of the brook. But the gods took his net and dragged the brook, and Loki, finding he must be caught, tried to leap over the net; but Thor, another son of Odin and god of thunder, war, and strength, caught him by the tail and compressed it, so the salmons ever since have had that part remarkably fine and thin. They bound him with chains and suspended a serpent over his head, whose venom falls upon his face drop by drop. His wife, Siguna, sits by his side and catches the drops as they fall in a cup; but when she carries it away to empty it, the venom falls upon Loki, which makes him howl with horror, and twist his body about so violently that the whole earth shakes, and this produces what men call earthquakes.

In this Norse myth we have a splendid mixture of beliefs about what is possible and what it means to be alive, to be dead, to be powerful. One can almost hear Wagner's magnificent music throbbing in the background. Here the gods are anything but remote, moving easily between their special realm, the world of ordinary people, and the underworld of the dead. Although they are able to accomplish magical feats, they are subject to certain rules over which they have no control. There is an intriguing mixture here of violence, compassion, guile, and valor. In this reality, being dead is not the end; it simply means you have to stay where you are sent and you can't come out and play with the others. Here is a world of exuberant activity and boundless energy, much like a college town on the weekend of the big game. With gods such as these, no wonder mere mortals could build gigantic boats and sail off to the West into uncharted waters! The pious Christian settlements along the coastline of the British Isles and Europe were no match for this level of ferocity.

In the Norse world, the gods are careful to consult all forms of life, including "earths, and stones, and trees, and metals." Nothing is to be left out, and when it is, we see the dire consequences. Evil, in the form of Loki, steps in and uses the neglected mistletoe for his own nefarious purposes. But even Loki is finally captured and made to pay for his wickedness.

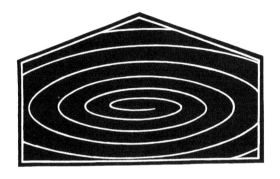

AFTER DEATH

Dear God, What is it like to die? I just want to know about it, I don't want to do it.

CHILDREN'S LETTERS TO GOD

The cynic might argue that all the stories people have been telling one another over the centuries about life after death are merely illusionary attempts to distract themselves from the truth that death is the irrevocable end to the wondrous, challenging, confusing, frightening, magnificent experience we call life. Perhaps this is so, we cannot know the absolute truth about life and death; we can only hold opinions. But we can take a look at the rich heritage of material that we have inherited describing all manner of complex worlds, which may or may not exist beyond planet Earth.

The stories in this section address the questions that lie just beneath the surface of consciousness for many of us, "What will happen when I die?"or the child's wondering, "Where do we go when we die?"

At the Gate of Gehinnom

Medieval Jewish: Midrash

Rabbi Joshua ben Levi said, "Once upon a time I was walking on my way, when I met the Prophet Elijah. He said to me, 'Would you like to be brought to the gate of Gehinnom?' I answered, 'Yes!' So he showed me men hanging by their hair, and he said to me, 'These were the men that let their hair grow to adorn themselves for sin.' Others were hanging by their eyes; these were they that followed their eyes to sin, and did not set the Holy Blessed One before them. Others were hanging by their noses; these were they that perfumed themselves to sin. Others were hanging by their tongues; these were they that had slandered. Others were hanging by their hands, these were they that had stolen and robbed. Others were hanging ignominiously; these were they that had committed adultery. Others were hanging by their feet; these were they that had run to sin. He showed me women hanging by their breasts; these were they that had uncovered their breasts for men, to make them sin.

"He showed me further men that were fed on fiery coals; these were they who had blasphemed. Others were forced to eat bitter gall; these were they that ate on fast days.

"He showed me further men eating fine sand; they are forced to eat it, and their teeth are broken; and the Holy Blessed One says to them, 'O you sinners! when you used to eat that which you stole and robbed it was sweet in your mouth; now you are

The Chronicles of Jerahmeel, edited and translated by Moses Gaster, (New York: Ktav, 1971) originally published in 1899. Used with permission.

not able to eat even this,' as it is said, 'You have broken the teeth of the wicked.' (Psalm 3:8)

"He showed me further men who were thrown from fire to snow, and from snow to fire; these were they that abused the poor who come to them for assistance; therefore are they thus punished, as it is said, 'You have caused men to ride over our heads; we went through fire and through water.' He showed me others that were driven from mountain to mountain, as a shepherd leads the flock from one mountain to another. Of these speaks the verse: 'Like sheep they are appointed to Sheol; death shall be their shepherd; and the upright shall have the dominion over them in the morning; and their form shall waste away in Sheol, leaving behind their dwelling.' " (Psalm 49:15)

Rabbi Yohanan said, "For every sin there is an angel appointed to obtain the expiation thereof; one comes first and obtains his expiation, then follows another and so on until all the sins are expiated. As with a debtor who has many creditors, and who come before the king to claim their debts, and the king delivers him to them, and says, 'Take him and divide him between yourselves,' so also is the soul delivered in Gehinnom to cruel angels, and they divide it among themselves."

Rabbi Joshua ben Levi, is a familiar character in Jewish texts, appearing in a number of descriptions of heaven and hell. He is able to travel to the underworld much as the Greek, Roman, and Norse gods can, even though he is alive. In the medieval period, in the Christian as well as the Jewish tradition, there were numerous elaborate depictions of what happened after death to those who misbehaved, Dante's *Inferno* being perhaps the best known.

The House of the Dead

Babylonian: Ancient Middle East

Once upon a time, the people of Babylon, thought the earth to be in the form of a great hemisphere. Its hollow interior was filled with the waters of the Deep, upon which it also rested. The layer of earth was a crust of solid ground, thought to be of great thickness. Deep down below the surface of this crust, which formed the "mountain of the World," was a great cavern called Arallu. In this cavern was the great House of the Dead, surrounded by seven walls; these were so strongly built and so heavily guarded by beings of the underworld that no one who had once entered therein could ever hope to return again to earth; indeed another name for the underworld was "The Land of No Return." The House of the Dead was dark and gloomy, and in it the dead dragged out a weary and miserable existence. They never beheld the light of the sun but sat in unchanging gloom. In appearance they resembled birds, for they were clothed in garments of feathers; their only food was dust and mud, and over everything thick dust was scattered. The goddess who presided over this joyless realm of the dead was named Allatu.

One day, the god Nergal, seeking revenge for past insults, decided to journey to Arallu with the intention of slaying Allatu. So he set out alone and fought his way into the lower world, until he came to the first of the seven walls; it was guarded by serpent-headed men in long tunics. Concealing himself behind a large boulder, he

Adapted and expanded from material in *Babylonian Religion and Mythology,* by L.W. King, pp. 34–43 (London: Kegan Paul International, 1903).

He could feel her jet black eyes burning into his brain
as though they were reading his very thoughts.

took out a kind of flute and started to play a haunting melody. Such sounds had never before been heard in the land of the dead. The serpent guards were at first astonished, then watchful, finally transfixed by the unfamiliar eerie sound. Nergal continued to play as he came out, ever so slowly, from behind the boulder. Like an afternoon shadow, he glided past the first wall and the entranced serpent demons.

The second wall was guarded by a pair of bird demons, men with the heads of eagles. While still some distance off, Nergal stooped down and picked up a small stone, placed it in his slingshot, and fired it high into the air. It landed right at the bird demons' feet. Together they gazed skyward to see from whence it came. Another stone fell, just missing the guard on the left. A third glanced off the beak of the right-hand guard. As the eagle demons craned their necks looking up, Nergal raced past them undetected.

At the third wall, guards with the heads of horses marched back and forth in tight formation. Nergal lay down on the ground, took in a giant breath, and slowly blew it out in the direction of the guards. A great thick cloud of dust arose and covered the horse demons so that they could neither see nor breathe. Choking and sputtering, they milled about in confusion as Nergal passed by unnoticed.

When he approached the fourth wall, Nergal could see it was guarded by ram-headed demons. Moving steadily forward in full view of the guards, he clapped his hands and shouted to attract their attention. When they saw him coming, the ram demons all lowered their heads and charged straight at the intruder. Nergal quickened his stride, and just as the guards were about to reach him, he stretched out his hands, grabbed the horns of the closest ram demon, and vaulted over him in a graceful somersault. Landing on his feet, he found himself inside the fourth wall.

At the fifth wall a huge guard with the head of a bear waited. Nergal drew his two-edged sword and challenged the demon to fight. Back and forth they dueled for some time, neither gaining an advantage. Finally Nergal saw an opening and taking a mighty lunge, ran his sword through the heart of the bear demon. Before leaving his vanquished foe, he reached into the demon's chest and pulled out the severed heart and liver and carried them with him past the fifth wall.

The sixth wall was guarded by men with the heads of hounds. Nergal could see from afar they were ravenous with hunger; their tongues hung out as they sniffed the air for any scent of food. Pulling the still-dripping heart and liver from beneath his cloak, he hurled them with all his might so that they landed a short distance from where the hound demons were stationed. When they caught the scent of fresh meat, they all converged on it at once, baying horribly as they tore at the flesh and fought with one another for the last morsels. Nergal strode safely past the snarling guards, washed the blood off his hands in the moat, and continued on his way.

At the seventh wall he encountered the fiercest guards of all: a pair of giant men with the heads of lions. When they saw Nergal coming, they drew together barring his passage. Nergal marched right up to them and demanded, "Which one of you is the chief guard here? I have a very important message for the chief."

"We are equal here; state your message," came the answer.

Nergal shook his head gravely. "I have been told that one of you is stronger, more powerful, and therefore more important than the other. I must deliver my message only to that one." The lion demons stared down at Nergal; then they looked suspiciously at each other. Could it be true, that one was more important than the other? Such a thought had never occurred to either of them before. Slowly they began to circle one another, watching closely for any signs of weakness. Each knew he was certainly the stronger, more powerful, and therefore more important one. Throwing off their tunics, they made a great show of muscle to prove their strength; each lion demon roared a mighty roar to demonstrate his power; each tossed his huge head to indicate importance. Nergal watched as their mood gradually shifted from mere audacity to fiery rage. Suddenly, with fangs flashing and guttural snarls, they lunged toward each other, each in a fierce attempt to best the other. Down in the dust they fell, locked in mortal struggle. Nergal stepped around them, passed the seventh and final wall, and soon found himself at the portal of the House of the Dead.

Here he encountered not a demon but the god Nedu. "What is your business here, stranger?" inquired Nedu.

"I am no stranger," replied Nergal, "but a god, like yourself, come with an important message for your mistress, Queen Allatu. Let me pass."

"Not so fast," snapped Nedu. "How did you get past all my guards at the seven walls? No one is allowed through without my permission."

"Ah," replied Nergal, "that is because they were wise enough to recognize me and perceive the importance of my mission to Allatu. They hastened me on my way and assured me that you, who are far wiser than they could ever hope to be, would do the same." Nedu could hardly argue with this last statement, so stepping aside and putting his hand on the great door knob, he bowed and ushered Nergal inside the House of the Dead.

At first Nergal wandered from room to room in search of Allatu. He knew that when he found her, he would have to act quickly and deftly if he was to accomplish his mission. Suddenly, turning a corner, he came face-to-face with a creature so ugly the mere sight of him took Nergal's breath away. "Who are you and what do you want?" hissed the grisly, misshapen being.

"You should know that I am the god Nergal and I have come with an important message for Allatu. Tell me where she is to be found," bluffed Nergal. "Who are you, miserable one, to bar my way?" he added, glaring fiercely at the winged monster.

"I am Namtar, chief minister to Allatu," came the boastful reply. "I am Allatu's messenger and carry out all her orders." He made an awkward bowing gesture. "Most especially I enjoy," the watery red eyes darted right and left, "bringing pestilence and disease to people on earth." A hideous cackle emerged from his twisted mouth. Then he turned abruptly and struggled up a long flight of stone stairs, hissing over his shoulder as he went, "Follow me."

When they reached the top, they were at one end of a long gallery. Nergal could make out two figures, both women, seated at the far end. "There!" Namtar pointed a wart-covered, clawlike finger down the hall "There is the one you seek. Now I must be about my business. I have a sack of plague to deliver to earth before sundown."

Nergal walked slowly down the dimly lit gallery, wondering to himself which of the women was Allatu. He sensed his greatest challenge now lay ahead of him. As he drew closer, he could see that one of the women was writing down on a tablet what the other one was saying. The speaker had her back to Nergal, and the scribe sat close to a narrow window where a pale light filtered into the gloom of the lengthy gallery. "And I further decree that for the next year all my demons, under the direction of my faithful Namtar, shall work vigilantly to see that disease is spread among mankind so that I can have fresh subjects to rule in my domain. Those who fail to carry out this order.... Why do you not write, Belittseri?" The speaker turned to see what had captured her scribe's attention.

"Who are you and how did you gain access to my inner chamber?" Nergal could see at once that this was Allatu, the goddess he had come to slay. He stared at her long and hard before he spoke. He had expected that the ruler of the lower world would be a commanding personage. What he had not anticipated, however, was the force of her presence; with the head of a lioness and the body of a woman, she somehow conveyed an intensely striking beauty. In her lap she fondled several serpents with her long slender hands. Here was a queen to be reckoned with, Nergal thought. He could feel her jet black eyes burning into his brain as though they were reading his very thoughts.

"I am Nergal and I come to bring you greetings from the gods of the upper world," he began, taking a broad stance in front of Allatu, who continued to finger her serpents without ever taking her eyes from her visitor. Glancing at the scribe, Belittseri, he continued. "The message I carry is for your ears alone." At these words, Belittseri, pale in comparison to the queen but a goddess in her own right with intuitive powers, arose, bowed to Allatu and Nergal, and silently made her way along the gallery, departing down the stone stairs.

"So, what is this message you bring?" inquired Allatu evenly.

Nergal knew he must not linger but move quickly if he was to carry out his dreadful mission. "The time has come for you to leave this kingdom. Your reign is over!" As he spoke these words, he drew his mighty sword, took two steps toward Allatu, and twisting his wrist, prepared to strike with all his strength on the side of her neck. Just as the blade came forward, within inches of its target, the serpents lying in Allatu's lap shot out and wrapped themselves around Nergal's hand. Instantly his arm was frozen in midair.

"That would be very foolish of you, killing me." Allatu remained seated as she spoke quietly, never taking her eyes from Nergal's face. "You see, if I were to die, all of my ministers, guards and other demons would turn on you at once and tear you apart, limb from limb. No, I have a far better plan." She rose from her seat, moved toward the little window, and beckoned Nergal to join her there. "See out there," she waved her hand across the horizon. "If you kill me, you will surely die as well and all this will be lost to us. Stay here, become my partner and husband and I will share my Realm of the Dead with you forever."

Nergal had been so stunned by the sudden turn of events, he could only drop his sword, releasing the serpents, who slid onto the floor, and follow Allatu to gaze out of the window. He felt his rage draining out of him as he stood next to her. His reason for making this arduous journey of revenge melted away like the morning mist. Looking over Allatu's shoulder, he could see scores of feather-clad dead souls wandering about in the dust and beyond them the seven walls past which he had so recently maneuvered. "Think of the power you can have here. All of my ministers, guards, and demons will obey your every command after you and I are married." Allatu had turned from the window and was standing a few inches from Nergal, her hypnotic gaze trained on him once more. She placed one hand gently on his arm. "You will be greatly honored as King of the Dead and you will have power over all mankind."

And so it was that Allatu and Nergal came to rule over the realm of the dead with all their ministers, guards, and demons carrying out their orders and daily bringing them fresh subjects from the land of the living. The Babylonians, for their part, made sure to bury their dead with messages and offerings to Allatu and Nergal, thereby assuring them a safe passage to the underworld.

This story is based on a slim description by L. R. King of the Babylonians' beliefs about the afterworld. While I have fabricated the details of this adventure, the basic facts, the characters, their roles, and the conditions in the "Land of No Return," are from original documents. According to King, " The Babylonians had no hope of a joyous life beyond the grave, and they did not conceive a paradise in which the deceased would live a life similar to that lived upon earth. They made no distinction between the just and the unjust, the good and the bad, but believed that all would share a common fate and be reduced to the same level after death."[†]

How different this view seems from many other traditions, including the familiar Judeo-Christian beliefs that place emphasis on accountability in this life determining our fate in the afterlife!

[†] King, L. W., Babylonian Religion and Mythology (London: Kegan, Paul, Trench, Trubner, & Co., Ltd. 1903) pp. 35–36.

The Many Fearful Hells

Hindu: India

Some folk say there are many fearful hells: awful provinces with instruments of torture and with fire into which are hurled all those who are addicted when alive to sinful practices.

The man who bears false witness through partiality or who utters any falsehood, plunders a town, kills a cow, or strangles a man goes to the Hell of Obstruction.

The murderer of a Brahman (high-caste person), stealer of gold, or drinker of wine goes to Swine Hell as does anyone who associates with him.

The murderer of a fellow citizen, and the one who is guilty of adultery with the wife of his spiritual teacher, is sentenced to the Padlock Hell.

The one who holds an incestuous relationship with a sister or who murders an ambassador goes to the Hell of the Heated Caldron.

The seller of his wife, a goader, a horse-dealer, and one who deserts his adherents falls into the Red Hot Iron Hell.

He who commits incest with his daughter-in-law or a daughter is cast into the Hell of the Great Flame.

He who is disrespectful of his spiritual guide, who is abusive of his betters, who reviles the Laws or who sells them, who associates with women in a prohibited degree goes into Salt Hell.

Adapted from *The Vishnu Purana, A System of Hindu Mythology and Tradition,* translated from the Sanscrit by H. H. Wilson, pp. 206–211 (London: John Murray, 1840).

A thief and a scorner of prescribed observances falls into the Place of Bewildering.

He who hates his father, the Brahmans, and the gods, or who spoils precious gems is punished in the Hell Where the Worms Are His Food.

He who practices magic rites for the harm of others is hurled into the Hell of Insects.

The vile wretch who eats his meal before offering food to the gods or to the guests falls into the Hell Where Saliva Is Given for Food.

The maker of arrows is sentenced to the Piercing Hell.

The maker of lances, swords, and other weapons goes to the dreadful Hell called Murderous.

He who takes unlawful gifts, offers sacrifices to improper objects, or observes the stars for the prediction of events is sent to the Head-Inverted Hell.

He who eats by himself sweetmeats mixed with his rice, and a Brahman who sells milk, flesh, liquors, sesame, or salt or who commits violence falls into the Hell Where Matter Flows, as do they who rear cats, cocks, goats, dogs, hogs, or birds.

Public performers, fishermen, the follower of one born in adultery, a prisoner, an informer, one who lives by his wife's prostitution, one who attends to affairs on the day of the full or new moon, an incendiary, a treacherous friend, a soothsayer, and those who sell the acid used in sacrifices go to the Hell Whose Wells Are of Blood.

He who destroys a beehive or pillages a hamlet is condemned to yet another Hell.

He who causes impotence, trespasses on others' lands, is impure, or who lives by fraud, is punished in Black Hell.

He who wantonly cuts down trees goes to a Hell Where the Leaves of the Trees Are Swords.

A tender of sheep, a hunter of deer, a potter goes to the Hell termed the Fiery Flame.

The violator of a vow and one who breaks the rules of his order falls into the Hell of Pincers.

The religious student who sleeps in the day and is, though unconsciously, defiled, and they who, though mature, are instructed in sacred literature by their children receive punishment in the Hell Where They Feed Upon Dogs.

These hells and hundreds of thousands of others are the places in which sinners pay the penalty of their crimes. As numerous as are the offenses that men commit, so many are the hells in which they are punished: and all who deviate from the duties imposed upon them by their class and condition, whether in thought, word, or deed, are sentenced to punishment in the regions of the damned.

The gods in heaven are beheld by the inhabitants of hell, as they move with their heads inverted, whilst the gods, as they cast their eyes downward, behold the sufferings of those in hell.

The various stages in existence are: inanimate things, fish, birds, animals, men, holy men, gods, and liberated spirits; each in succession is a thousand degrees superior to that which precedes it. Through these steps the beings that are either in heaven or in hell are destined to proceed, until final emancipation be obtained. That is, when punishment or reward in hell or heaven, proportional to the sin or virtue of the individual, has been received, he must be born again as a stone or a plant, and gradually migrate through the several inferior conditions, until he is once more born a man. His future state is then in his own power. That sinner goes to hell who neglects the due expiation of his guilt.

These terse yet vivid descriptions of the consequences of sinful behavior come directly from ancient Hindu tradition. One could compare and contrast them with more familiar Christian and Jewish texts about the afterlife. A different, and perhaps more rewarding task, however, would be to imagine how one might live one's life if "The Many Fearful Hells" were a conscious part of one's belief system. Hinduism is the oldest of the currently extant mainstream religions, but it is not well understood by those reared in Judeo-Christian traditions in the West. The idea that even the most despicable being can work his or her way back toward redemption and eventual enlightenment, is intriguing. In the West we say we believe in redemption, but often our behavior indicates otherwise.

The Wondrous Land of Magh Mar

Celtic: Ancient Ireland

There, there is neither "mine" nor "thine";

White are teeth there, dark the brows;

A delight of the eye the array of our hosts;

Every cheek there is of the hue of the foxglove.

Purple the surface of every plain,

A marvel of beauty the blackbird's eggs;

Though the Plain of Fal be fair to see,

'Tis desolate once you have known Magh Mar.

Fine though you think the ale of Ireland,

More exhilarating still is the ale of Tir Mar;

A wondrous land is the land I tell of,

Youth does not give way to age there.

Sweet warm streams flow through the land,

The choice of mead and of wine;

Splendid people without blemish,

Conception without sin, without lust.

In *Celtic Mythology,* by Proinsias MacCana, p.125 (Middlesex, England: Newnes Books, 1985). Permission applied for.

Descriptions of the other world by early Irish poets vary widely but have a number of elements in common. They are heavily laced with fanciful magic, paradox, lyricism, and reckless bravery. The appeal here is in the disarming way the poet intertwines concern with practical matters — good teeth, good ale — and romantic images — purple plains, sweet warm streams. The invitation to this other world seems irresistible.

The Celts wandered westward across Europe, some settling in Brittany, others moving on to the British Isles, where they eventually settled mostly in Wales and Ireland. Renowned for their storytelling since pre-Christian times, it is no wonder the Celts' bardic tradition gave rise to the many Arthurian legends.

In his Celtic Mythology, Proinsias MacCana comments, "Nothing about the Celts is more certain than that they believed in a life after death; . . . this belief was part of the formal teaching of the Gaulish druids . . . . The Celts accept death without trepidation, since it is for them only a juncture in a long life."[†]

[†] MacCana, Proinsias, *Celtic Mythology* (Middlesex, England: Newnes Books, 1985), p.122.

The Garden of Eden

Rabbinic Jewish: The Talmud

The Garden of Eden has two gates of ruby, by which stands six myriads of ministering angels. The luster of the face of each of them glistens like the splendor of the firmament. When a righteous person arrives, they divest him in white robes of the clouds of glory, set two crowns upon his head, one made of gems and pearls and the other of gold . . . place eight myrtles in his hand and praise him saying: "Go eat your food in joy." They take him into a place where are brooks of water, surrounded by eight hundred varieties of roses and myrtles. Each person has a chamber allotted to him according to the honor due him. From it issues four streams, one of milk, one of wine, one of balsam, and one of honey; and above every chamber there is a golden vine studded with thirty pearls, each one of them glistening like the brilliance of the planet Venus.

In every corner of the Garden of Eden there are eighty myriad species of trees, the most inferior of them being finer than all the aromatic plants [of this world]; and in each corner are sixty myriads of ministering angels singing in pleasant tones. In the center is the Tree of Life, its branches covering the whole of the Garden of Eden, containing five hundred thousand varieties of fruit all differing in appearance and taste. Above it are the clouds of glory, and it is smitten by four winds so that its odor is wafted from one end of the world to the other. Beneath it are the disciples of the sages who expounded the Torah, each of them possessing two chambers, one of the stars and the other of the sun and moon. Between every chamber hangs a curtain of glory, behind which lies Eden.

Everyman's Talmud, edited by Abraham Cohen, (New York: Schocken Books, Inc. 1975). Permission applied for.

Simcha Paull Raphael believes this description probably dates from the thirteenth century. Here are his comments. "What we find in this text is a specific concern with the content of the supernal worlds, and less of an emphasis on the ethics of reward and punishment . . . . For those who claim that Judaism does not have a concern with the details of the afterlife, this particular text, and the tradition that it spawns, is a direct contradiction."[†]

[†] Raphael, Simcha Paull, *Jewish Views of the Afterlife* (Northvale, N.J.: Jason Aronson, 1994), p.154.

Gourd Woman

Native American: The Kogi of Northern Colombia

Some folk say that when a person dies, his or her soul, a tiny, invisible replica of the person, stands poised just inside the person's mouth. The mouth is carefully held open by friends so that a green fly, sent by the Great Mother, can enter and carry off the soul to begin its wanderings in the Land of the Dead. This is the story of what happened to one such soul called Moad.

The green fly deposited Moad at the base of a steep, winding mountain trail and then departed. Moad started to climb, but she hadn't gone far when she heard a rumbling sound from above. Glancing up, she saw a rock shower descending as if from the sky and barely had time to duck behind a boulder to avoid being crushed. With a mighty crash the rocks landed and scattered on the path just where Moad had been standing a moment earlier. Moad peeked out from her shelter, then hearing no more rumblings, cautiously continued climbing.

The climb was arduous, but Moad persevered until, rounding a corner, she suddenly encountered a gaping crevasse. One more step and she would have fallen to the center of the earth! Beyond the crevasse Moad could see the path continuing up the mountain, but how to get across was a mystery. To the right, the mountain dropped away thousands of feet; to the left, a sheer rock face stretched straight up into the clouds. Moad knew there was no turning back, so she sat down to figure out a solution.

Adapted and expanded from "Some Kogi Models of the Beyond," by G. Reichel-Dolmatoff, *Journal of Latin American Lore,* 10:1 (1984) pp. 65–67 (Los Angeles: University of California). Copyright © Regents of the University of California. Used with permission.

Gourd Woman never deserted Moad, offering consolation and comfort,
as she stood before Death to be judged on even the smallest transgressions.

Feeling very small and lonely in this perilous dilemma, Moad was startled by a huge yellow wasp that dove out of the sky and with a fearful hissing sound headed straight for her head. Jumping up to avoid the oncoming wasp, she flattened herself along the cliff to her left. The yellow wasp continued to dive; Moad could see its enormous eyes glaring at her; the hissing became louder and louder. Moad closed her eyes and braced herself for the anticipated pain from the wasp's giant stinger. Instead she felt the brush of the wasp's wing on her cheek and heard ringing in her ears the rasping message, "Hurry, hurry!" Then silence.

Moad opened her eyes and looked around; the wasp had vanished. She became aware of the cold rock at her back. Turning to examine it more closely, she noticed a thin crack that stretched away up the mountain at a slight incline. Perhaps this was a way to get across the crevasse. Using the crack as a hand hold and with her feet dangling unsupported, Moad, carefully and ever so slowly, inched her way along the cliff, not daring to look at the gaping chasm below. When she reached the other side and sensed it was safe to let go, she slid down the rock face and landed on the path in an exhausted heap. She wanted nothing more than to rest there, but from a distance she heard the ominous hissing sound approaching, so she scrambled up and continued on her journey.

Many more hazards crossed her path as she made her way up the mountain. Each time she felt discouraged or stopped to rest, the giant yellow wasp swooped down to plague her and drive her onward. More than once she felt its dreaded sting. And always in her ear she heard the shrill command, "Hurry, hurry!"

Finally Moad reached the high mountains, where the air was crisp and cool. Then, without warning, in front of her on the path there appeared several tall figures covered from head to foot in midnight blue. "Who are these strange creatures?" wondered Moad silently.

"We are the Messengers of Death," came the answer, though no words were spoken. "Tell us your name and describe your background." Moad found she was able to communicate telepathically with the Messengers of Death. When she finished telling about her family and village life, the Messengers moved away and consulted amongst themselves. Moad could see them gesticulating in different directions and shaking their heads, sometimes indicating "yes" and sometimes "no." At last they returned to face Moad. "This is the route you must take. Pay careful attention and don't forget anything we tell you." With that warning the Messengers of Death conveyed to Moad lengthy and detailed instructions as to the precise way she was to proceed. Then, without further ado, they were gone.

"I hope I can remember all this," worried Moad as she set off on the next part of her journey. She trudged along repeating the Messengers' instructions over and over in her head until she came to the banks of a swift-flowing river. For some time she walked up and down the shore searching for a bridge or at least stepping stones to help her across. "I wonder what this river is called," thought Moad. No sooner had the thought formed in her mind than she heard a voice in her head reply, "This is the River of Death."

Moad was beginning to think there was no way across the River of Death when a dog suddenly appeared. "Give me your jawbone," he demanded.

"Why should I give up my precious jawbone?" asked Moad.

"If you do, I will help you across the river. If you don't, you will be stuck here forever." Moad remembered the warning of the Messengers of Death and the stings of the yellow wasp, so she gave up her jawbone, and the dog carried her safely across the river on his back.

After a short time she came to a second river. The voice in her head promptly announced, "This is called the River of Tears."

"Why is it called the River of Tears?" wondered Moad.

"Because it is swollen with the tears of the bereft, the people you have left behind."

"What do I do now?" worried Moad.

"Wait," came the answer. So Moad sat down by the side of the River of Tears to wait. For a time it continued its strong flow, and Moad knew she could never venture across. Little by little, however, the waters began to recede until finally she saw a series of stepping stones appear and realized at last she could make her way across without being washed downstream.

"One more river to go," said the voice in Moad's head as she scrambled out of the River of Tears. Sure enough, a third river awaited her not far off. "This one is called the River of the Sun," she was told. As Moad stood staring into the swirling waters of the River of the Sun, she heard a footstep behind her. She turned around to find a little old woman, dressed in rags standing there.

"What is your name and where do you come from?" demanded the little old woman, eyeing her sharply. Moad repeated the same information she had given the Messengers of Death. The woman listened intently, and when Moad had concluded, turned on her heel saying, "Follow me." Moad obeyed but she couldn't help thinking, "Something is familiar about this person. Where could I have met her before?" The little old woman came to a spot along the riverbank where there was a narrow pebble beach. There, tied to a nearby bush, bobbed a tiny round boat with two paddles.

"Hop in," ordered the little old woman. "No time to dawdle." Moad stepped gingerly into the boat and sat down on the only seat next to her guide. "Start paddling. The current's mighty swift along this shore," she warned. For several minutes Moad concentrated all her strength on maneuvering the boat out of the current and toward the other shore. At last she felt the pressure of the water beneath them lessen and rested her oar for a moment, turning to her companion. Moad could hardly believe her eyes! Seated next to her was no longer the figure of a little old woman clothed in rags but her very own mother with her familiar smile and sparkling eyes. Moad's mother laughed gently when she saw her daughter's look of astonishment. "It's a lucky thing you treated me well during my lifetime, child, or you wouldn't be receiving my help across this River of the Sun right now." Moad placed her paddle in the bottom of the boat and threw her arms around her mother, thanking her for all her help, not only now but in her whole past lifetime as well.

"But what would have happened if I had mistreated you, Mother?" Moad wanted to know.

"I should have summoned one of Death's Messengers, who would have sent you off on an evil path," replied her mother. Moad shuddered at the memory of the stern figures in midnight blue. "Now, out you go and be on your way," chided the woman. Having reached the far shore, the little boat came to a gentle stop. Moad scrambled out and up the riverbank. When she turned to wave good-bye to her mother and the trusty little craft, they were nowhere to be seen. The River of the Sun, however, true to its name, sparkled so brightly, that Moad was forced to cover her eyes and turn away. Just as she did, she heard the faint peal of a familiar laugh.

Moad followed a path that led away from the river and soon found herself standing at the door of a great temple. As she gazed up at the elaborate stone work, the door slowly swung open. Moad entered a large room where many priests and chiefs were gathered. "Nine days and nights have passed since your death," intoned the chief priest, stepping forward. "What do you have to say for yourself?" Moad was astonished to learn she had been traveling for so long, having lost all track of time. She couldn't think how to answer the chief priest, so she dropped her head and was silent. As she looked down at her feet and legs, she realized they were literally worn to the bone from her struggles, though curiously she felt no pain. The priests and chiefs conferred among themselves, consulting documents and glancing in Moad's direction from time to time.

At last they turned and faced little Moad, who had continued to stand forlornly in the center of the great temple. The chief priest cleared his throat and fixed his eyes sternly on Moad. "We are now prepared to pass judgment on you, Moad, and send you on the next part of your journey. So far you have conducted yourself with courage and fortitude. Your trials, however, have only just begun. From here you shall proceed to the first of the Nine Villages of Death, where you will be accused and judged for all your sins and misdemeanors committed on earth. Since we see from the records your cause of death was heart failure, we are sending you first to the Village of the Heart." Moad nodded her head bravely, even though she was feeling far from brave. She turned and started to leave. "Wait!" boomed the chief priest, holding up one hand. Moad turned back, wondering what she might have forgotten. Then from behind the priests and chiefs stepped a woman clad in the softest garment Moad had ever seen. As she came toward Moad, her garment seemed to change color with her every movement. Moad, sensing she was in the presence of a true friend, felt her spirits lift.

"I will be your companion on your travels," said the woman placing her arm gently on Moad's shoulder. Moad looked up and smiled at the woman.

"My name is Moad," she said. "What shall I call you?"

"People call me Gourd Woman," came the answer.

The two bade farewell to the priests and chiefs, left the temple, and set out for the Village of the Heart. For the next twenty years they wandered through the Nine Villages of Death, where Moad was accused and judged for all her sins and misdemeanors committed on earth.

"For pushing your sister out of the hammock: three copper coins."

"For laziness: one month scrubbing floors."

"For disobeying your mother: two silver coins and no dinner for a week."

"For telling a lie to your husband: a diet of bitter herbs."

"For speaking harshly to your child: four days of silence."

"For envying your neighbor's good fortune: seven silver coins and ten days hauling rocks."

There were times when the list of Moad's transgressions seemed endless and she grew despondent. During the whole ordeal, however, she had the companionship of Gourd Woman. Moad found her to be the most precious companion imaginable because it was Gourd Woman's job to speak up in defense of Moad and pay any fines that were imposed. In addition, Gourd Woman never deserted Moad, offering consolation and comfort, as she stood before Death to be judged on even the smallest transgressions.

In addition to Gourd Woman, there were three priests and their wives who acted as Moad's counsel. Knowing that she was not alone made this part of her journey bearable. If she was found guilty, she had to stay in the village for a certain number of years, where she was punished by Death's henchmen. Gourd Woman, however, stood by her throughout.

The day finally came when Moad had redeemed all her sins and settled the last misdemeanor so that she could pass out of the Nine Villages of Death and arrive at last on the highest mountain peak called Brother Snow. This pleasant land, devoid of all illness, she discovered, was called the Land of the Mother. At its very center was a great temple and surrounding the temple, many villages, where Moad found a final resting place. It wasn't long before she was settled in a comfortable home, with plenty of food, a warm hearth, a hammock, and, yes, Gourd Woman preparing a nourishing meal.

Here, as in Dante's *Inferno*, death is just the beginning of a journey. Dante's Mount Purgatory, in the Kogi story resembles the Kogi's own Sierra Madre de Santa Marta.

There are a number of familiar elements here: the arduous journey, being judged, crossing water, atoning for past sins. What is different and certainly appealing is the figure of Gourd Woman, who, after Moad has passed her initial trials, stays with her and supports her throughout her long ordeal. Although, Christians speak of the Holy Spirit (one element of the Trinity) as the Comforter, and many can attest to its reassuring powers, so often we are told: You come into and go out of this world alone. Not so, according to the Kogi. Gourd Woman will never desert the soul. Maternal and compassionate, she is a compelling presence in the afterlife.

In the same article from which this story is taken, the anthropologist G. Reichel-Dolmatoff writes,

> The Kogi say that death is the inverse act to that of birth; it is the moment when the individual begins to return once more to the body of the Great Mother. Death, therefore, is not a tragic event but is the fulfillment of a long-cherished wish. Life is but a brief period between two intrauterine states, which determines the degree of gratification the soul will experience in the second state, according to the virtuousness of the person's conduct. It is only a period of trials, a task that has to be fulfilled. Old people who have arrived at this state of wisdom die in peace with themselves and the world. Their deaths do not affect the lives of those who remain; they do not cause great

lamentations or commotion, nor are lengthy rituals thought to be necessary. Just like birth, the death of a person concerns only his close family.[†]

The Kogi have an unusual culture in many ways. About eleven thousand strong, they have chosen to live in isolation in the Sierra Nevada de Santa Marta mountains of northern Colombia, resisting the influences of Western civilization for more than five hundred years. Thus they have kept their highly sophisticated spiritual belief system and way of life intact. Like the Tibetans (and certain other peoples), they believe everything is created on spiritual planes before it can manifest itself materially. The two cultures on opposite sides of the globe share other beliefs as well. For instance, the Kogi admonish family and friends not to weep for them when they die so their soul will not be detained at the River of Tears; the Tibetans say that crying and tears around a dying person's bedside are experienced by that person as thunder and hail.

In 1991 the Kogi, normally extremely reclusive, allowed British filmmaker Alan Ereira to make a film about them, *From the Heart of the World.* They had become so concerned about the state of the world, our abuse of the environment and of all forms of life, that they felt impelled to issue a warning to the rest of humanity, whom they call "the younger brother."

[†] Reichel-Dolmatoff, G., "Some Kogi Models of the Beyond," Journal of Latin American Lore (January 1984), p. 64.

The Day of Sorting Out

Muslim: The Qur'an

The Great News for man, in his spiritual Destiny,

Is the Judgment to come, the Day of Sorting Out.

Do not the Power, the Goodness, and the Justice

Of God reveal themselves in all nature? —

The Panorama around us, the voice in our souls,

And the harmony between heaven and earth?

That day is sure to arrive at its time

Appointed, when behold! the present order

Will pass away. Then will the Fruits

Of Evil appear, and the Fruits of Righteousness.

God's blessings will be more than the merits of men;

But who can argue with the Fountain of Grace?

And who can prevent the course of Justice?

Let us then, before it becomes too late,

Betake ourselves to our Lord Most Gracious!

The *Holy Qur'an,* translation and commentary by Abdullah Yusef Ali, Sura 78, p.1671 (Beirut, Lebanon: Dar Al Arabia, 1938.)

There are a number of beautiful passages in the *Qur'an* dealing with the after-life and the day of judgment. One speaks of the coming of peace, another of full reality revealed, still another of the need for each soul to answer for itself. This passage was chosen because it invites us to learn from nature, the world around us. Connection with nature, for many, has a special appeal in today's high-tech world of "virtual reality." In addition, the logic and imagery in the two questions: "But who can argue with the Fountain of Grace? And who can prevent the course of Justice?" are compelling.

The Happy Land
Buddhist

Many kinds of rivers flow along in this world system Sukhavati. There are great rivers there, one mile broad, and up to fifty miles broad and twelve miles deep. And all these rivers flow along calmly, their water is fragrant with manifold agreeable odors, in them there are bunches of flowers to which various jewels adhere, and they resound with various sweet sounds. And the sound which issues from these great rivers is as pleasant as that of a musical instrument, which consists of hundreds of thousands of kotis of parts, and which, skillfully played, emits a heavenly music. It is deep, commanding, distinct, clear, pleasant to the ear, touching the heart, delightful, sweet, pleasant, and one never tires of hearing it, it always agrees with one and one likes to hear it, like the words "Impermanent, peaceful, calm, and not-self." Such is the sound that reaches the ears of those beings.

And, Ananda, both the banks of those great rivers are lined with variously scented jewel trees, and from them bunches of flowers, leaves, and branches of all kinds hang down. And if those beings wish to indulge in sports full of heavenly delights on those riverbanks, then, after they have stepped into the water, the water in each case rises as high as they wish it to — up to the ankles, or the knees, or the hips, or their sides, or their ears. And heavenly delights arise. Again, if beings wish the water to be cold, for them it becomes cold; if they wish it to be hot, it becomes hot; if they wish it to be hot and cold, for them it becomes hot and cold, to suit their pleasure. And those rivers flow along, full of water scented with the finest odors, and covered with beautiful flowers, resounding with the sounds of many birds, easy to ford, free from mud, and with golden sand at the bottom. And all the wishes those beings may think of, they all will be fulfilled, as long as they are rightful.

"Description of the Happy Land," in *The Oxford Book of Death,* edited and compiled by D. J. Enright, translation by Edward Conze, p.181 (Oxford & New York: Oxford University Press, 1983). Permission applied for.

This story introduces the notion that individuals can choose what happens to them in the afterlife. How different this Buddhist scenario is from some of the others in which much emphasis is placed on an external judge (God) deciding the fate of the soul. Nevertheless, in case one is tempted to assume that "anything goes" in this Buddhist Happy Land, a caution seems appropriate. Perhaps the most important part of the passage comes at the very end: "And all the wishes those beings may think of, they will be fulfilled, as long as they are rightful." Concealed in the last simple phrase is a whole philosophy, a complete belief system. If there are rightful wishes, then presumably there are wrongful ones as well. So there is no getting away from personal accountability after all, even in a Happy Land, where rivers run hot and cold at will and jewel-covered flowers float on the water while heavenly music and agreeable odors fill the air.

The Four Ways of Death

Native American: The Aztecs of Mexico

Some folk say there are four ways people die. The first is the way of the warrior killed in battle. The warrior's soul, as it leaves the body, becomes an eagle and flies off to join in the feasting and dancing of the Heaven of the Sun. Every morning the eagles help to lift the Sun into the sky.

The second way of death is the ways of women who die in childbirth. Their souls are transformed into white doves and are allowed to take the Sun from high noon across the western sky and gently lower it down on the horizon. The souls of their babies are cradled among the leaves of the milk tree, which gives them mother's milk until it is time for them to return to earth to be born again.

The third way is that of people who drown or are struck by lightning. Their souls go to an earthly paradise in the West. There they live in the house of the Rain God, surrounded by flowers, turquoise and jade trees, and dancing rainbows from the mist.

Everyone else goes the fourth way to the Land of the Dead. This is a hard place to reach, requiring a journey of four years. First, the soul enters a wind tunnel, where, with deafening roar in its ears, it starts to descend. Down, down it falls into ever-increasing darkness. Suddenly, with a flash of steel, great knives appear on all sides; slashing and cutting with fury, they tear the flesh from its bones. The soul

Adapted from material in *Myths of Life & Death,* by C. A. Burland, pp. 135–137 (New York: Crown Publishers, ©1974). Used with permission.

emerges from that ordeal to find itself facing a terrible chasm. The only way across is on a rope as narrow as a knife's edge. The soul creeps along, clutching with hands and feet to keep from dropping into the abyss below. Once it has reached the other side of the chasm, the soul meets a red dog. "Take me with you," demands the red dog. Here the soul must decide whether or not it wants this companion on its journey. In either case, it next descends into yet another tunnel. This time it falls past clashing rocks, which threaten to crush it eternally if it does not jump through fast enough. If the soul had decided to take the red dog on its perilous journey, it encounters no danger; if not, it is doomed to certain annihilation.

Finally, if the soul makes it through all these hazards, it reaches the halls of the Death God, where everyone happily dances, sings, and feasts. The Death God, moving amongst the throng, picks up some of the souls and throws them into a central fire, whence, like sparks of light, they soar up to the Supreme God, who may, just may, decide to send them back to earth again.

Since the Aztecs developed complex and precise systems of mathematics and cosmology, it is not surprising to find their beliefs about the after-death equally explicit and detailed. It is interesting to note that warriors, regardless of their individual qualities, deeds, or misdeeds, are rewarded in death by being transformed into the powerful rulers of the skies: the eagle. For the Aztecs (as well as for many people today), dying in battle was considered a high honor. Similarly, women and babies who died in childbirth, a common occurrence in the Aztec world, are not subjected to the trials of ordinary folk. They too are celebrated in death; with their suffering behind them, they are elevated to the realm of the most honored. Both groups have given their lives for their people. The babies, being innocent, are simply nurtured and recycled back into life.

Those unfortunates who die from what people today might call acts of God are also exempt from further trauma; they are sent to the Aztec version of Club Med.

Everyone else meets a very different fate. The notion that the after-death journey is filled with trial and adventure is common. The Aztecs, however, take that sense of peril and drama to a level which a modern adventure story rarely attains.

The Day of Judgment

Christian: The Bible

Behold, I tell you a mystery;

We shall not all sleep, but we shall all be changed,

In a moment, in the twinkling of an eye, at the last trump:

For the trumpet shall sound,

And the dead shall be raised incorruptible,

And we shall be changed.

For this corruptible must put on incorruption,

And this mortal must put on immortality.

Then shall be brought to pass the saying that is written,

Death is swallowed up in victory.

O death where is thy sting?

O grave where is thy victory?

The sting of death is sin;

And the strength of sin is the law.

The *Bible*, King James translation, Corinthians, I, 15: 51–56.

As a devotee of Handel's *Messiah,* I never fail to be moved by this familiar passage from Corinthians. First the bass soloist thunders forth the mysterious good news of transformation; then the reedlike voices of alto and tenor intertwine with a duet both sweet and haunting.

The suggestion is that the human part of us all that is corruptible, or prone to error, will be transformed into our true spiritual essence. This, it seems to me is what the Stage Manager in *Our Town* is getting at when he talks about "that eternal part" waiting to "come out clear."

There is a wealth of material in the literature dealing with the last day of judgment from cultures and religions around the world; none, in my opinion, surpasses these simple words of Paul for sheer imagery and poetry.

The River

Native American: The Tlingit of Southern Alaska

Way up north, in the land of the northern lights, where the sun never sets in the summer and winter nights last for months, there once lived a man named Ebar, who hunted seal and walrus to feed his family.

One day while Ebar was off hunting, his kayak overturned in the icy waters. Down, down he went to the bottom of the sea. Then slowly he rose up to the surface again. When he climbed out of the water, Ebar found himself in a strange land. He began to walk, not knowing where he was going. He walked and walked until he was so tired he could walk no more. Ebar sat down under a large tree with spreading branches, some distance from a strong flowing river, and fell asleep. In the night, he was awakened briefly by a loud crash.

At the first light of dawn, Ebar could see that a piece of the riverbank had broken off and been swept away with the current. The next night his sleep was interrupted again by the same sound. Sure enough, in the morning he could see another piece of riverbank had vanished. Every night for nine nights a portion of the riverbank fell into the current with a crash. By now the edge of the river was so close, it was almost at his feet.

Ebar felt he could neither run away nor move. He was stuck there under that tree. On the tenth night the river current was stronger than usual. Ebar could see

Adapted from material in *Under Mount Saint Elias: The History & Culture of the Yakutat Tlingit,* by Frederica de Laguna, Smithsonian Contributions to Anthropology, vol 7, [in three parts] pp. 774–775 (Washington, D.C.: Smithsonian Institution Press, 1972).

down into the swirling waters. Suddenly there was a great rumbling sound; the riverbank broke away right under him and he fell into the stream. Ebar tried to cry out for help, but when he opened his mouth the sound of a newborn baby emerged. He looked up into familiar shining eyes. He was being gently held and rocked. A man no longer, he had been reborn as a baby among his own people.

The Tlingit live along the coast of southern Alaska. Life in the far north is harsh; people are often isolated for long periods by severe weather. Family ties, therefore, are all important and relationships are close. When a family member dies, it is not surprising that he or she should be thought of as being on a journey and eventually returning by way of water. This is, after all, what takes place in everyday life for coastal tribes, who depend on the sea for both transport and food.

Many cultures that believe in reincarnation have the soul returning to familiar surroundings. It helps those left behind in their process of grieving and letting go of a loved one to know that the spirit will return and be reborn in a new body to be loved and cherished once more.

In the Christian ritual of baptism, water is used as the vehicle for symbolic rebirth. Depending on the denomination, people have water touched on or poured over their heads or are totally immersed in water. They thereby become reborn as Christians and as such are eligible for the new life of the spirit. Chapter 3 of John's Gospel quotes Jesus as saying, "Except a man be born of water and of the Spirit, he cannot enter into the kingdom of God. That which is born of the flesh is flesh; and that which is born of the Spirit is spirit. Marvel not that I said unto thee, 'Ye must be born again.' The wind bloweth where it listeth, and thou hearest the sound thereof, but canst not tell whence it cometh, and whither it goeth: so is every one that is born of the Spirit."

In the nightly crumbling of the riverbank we can read the story of how death (or any transformation) chips away at the solid ground of our established, familiar sense of who we are. Sometimes ailing patients cling to their old habits and activities desperately, poignantly. One teenager with end-stage AIDS wanted to go rollerblading one last time, though he knew he was too weak. A trip to a rink was arranged. He spent only a few minutes on the skates and then gave it up with many sighs. He had to try — and fail — in order to convince himself that this chunk of riverbank had crumbled.

Viraf's Vision

Zoroastrian: Persia

Once, long ago in ancient Persia, there lived a righteous man named Viraf. One day after lunch, he sat down under a fig tree in his garden and fell asleep. Presently he found himself transported to a great marble hall that, without being told, he knew was called the House of Song. Here he saw three judges, Mithra, Sraosha, and Rashnu, presiding over a huge scale. One by one, the souls of the recently departed were led into the hall and made to stand before the judges. On the right side of the scale were placed all the good thoughts, words, and deeds of the deceased; on the left, all its evil thoughts, words, and deeds. No favor was shown on either side, either for the rich or for the poor, for the weak or for the strong. Every soul was judged entirely on its own life.

As Viraf watched, he could see that the good and evil thoughts, words, and deeds of the soul standing in front of the judges balanced the scales exactly. "Proceed to Hamestagan; the intermediate place of waiting, by way of the Chinvat Bridge." Mithra motioned to a door at the end of the hall where a guide waited to escort the soul on its way. Viraf followed along; they crossed over a narrow bridge and eventually came to a place where souls were divided into two groups. One group was shivering miserably from icy cold winds, while the other suffered from oppressive waves of heat. After a time the conditions were reversed. Those who had been cold were

Adapted from *Persian Mythology,* by John R. Hinnells, pp. 60–66 (London: The Hamlyn Publishing Group, Ltd., 1973). Permission applied for.

exposed to great heat and the over-heated found themselves freezing. "I wonder how long they have to endure that kind of punishment?" thought Viraf as he left Hamestagan, retraced his steps, and reentered the House of Song.

Here another soul was standing before the judges, and its good thoughts, words, and deeds far outweighed its evil ones. "This way." Sraosha pointed to the door. Again, Viraf followed close behind, curious about where this soul might be going. As they stepped outside the hall, a gentle, fragrant wind touched their faces, and they were greeted by a maiden more beautiful than Viraf had ever imagined.

"Who are you and where have you come from?" asked the astonished soul.

"I am the conscience of thine own self," replied the maiden. "The manifestation of all your good thoughts, words, and deeds. Come, I will lead you to the Chinvat Bridge. But first we must cross the River of Tears." Soon they came to a swift flowing stream and Viraf wondered how they might get across. "Does your family know the correct rituals to perform in your honor?" the maiden asked.

"Oh, yes," the soul assured her. "My family are always careful with prayers and ceremonies! I hope they haven't forgotten my warning against too many tears." As the soul spoke, the water level subsided a bit and a series of stepping stones appeared at intervals so that they were able to cross the stream safely. They continued on to the Chinvat Bridge, which Viraf noticed seemed much wider than before. Sraosha and other heavenly beings awaited to escort them across its broad expanse. When they were in the middle of the bridge, there suddenly appeared a host of twelve-foot-high heavenly beings, bearing a victorious Fire, which neither burned nor scorched but rather dispelled the darkness and purified the soul.

Once on the other side, the soul passed to the various stations of the heavens. First they went to the Star station. Here Viraf saw radiant souls sitting on magnificent thrones, glittering like the stars, splendid and full of glory. This, Viraf was told, is where good thoughts are received with hospitality. At the next station, the station of the Moon, they found those with whom good words find hospitality. The place felt peaceful and glowed with a soft silvery light. They moved on to the third station, that of the Sun, where they encountered a dazzling brilliance. Viraf discovered this is where good rulers are rewarded for their faithful administration of their heavy tasks. At the fourth station, Viraf and the soul were greeted by Vohu Manah, Good Mind, who led them into the presence of Ahura Mazda, the Divine One.

From this great vantage point Viraf was shown the different dwelling places of the righteous, those who were liberal, those who were faithful in the performance of their religion, and those women who had been good and faithful wives, considering their husbands as lords. Viraf was also shown the dwelling place of the farmers and artisans, of those who had carried out their work faithfully, together with the places of the shepherds, the heads of villages, teachers, religious seekers, and peace-seekers. Viraf saw that the souls all dwelt among fine carpets and cushions in great pleasure and joy.

Viraf thanked his guide, bade farewell to the righteous soul, and all at once found himself back in the House of Song, where yet another soul stood before the three judges. This time it was obvious that the evil thoughts, words, and deeds far outweighed the good ones. "What will happen now?" wondered Viraf.

Rashnu spoke up. "Take the door over there," he said sternly, indicating the same exit the others had taken. Once more Viraf followed behind. This time, however, when they stepped outside, they were choked by a foul stench and greeted by a naked, loathsomely diseased old hag. She stuck her face up close to the soul's.

"Know who I am?" she hissed. The soul shook its head in confusion. "I'm the manifestation of all your evil thoughts, words, and deeds!" She let out a horrible screech, grabbed the soul by the arm, and led it off muttering to herself. When they reached the River of Tears, Viraf was surprised to see it had become a raging torrent, with no stepping stones in sight. "Guess we'll just have to wait," snarled the old hag as she plunked herself down by the side of the stream. "Some folks carry on so about death, this river just about floods its banks." They waited by the rushing water for what seemed to Viraf like an eternity. Just when he had decided they would be stuck there forever, the old hag staggered up, got behind the soul, and with no warning whatsoever, pushed it into the current. Half swimming, half groping, with much stumbling and falling, they made their painful way across to the other shore. Viraf, not wanting to be left behind, followed as best he could.

When they reached the Chinvat Bridge, Viraf was appalled to see it was no longer the broad, solid structure he had encountered before but now appeared to be as narrow and sharp as a sword's edge. The old hag let out an ear-splitting scream, which turned into a blood-curdling howl as she transformed herself into a wild beast snapping and snarling at the soul's feet. The soul took three steps onto the knifelike bridge; one step of evil thoughts, one of evil words, and one of evil deeds. Then the wicked soul fell headlong into hell, crying and lamenting like a wolf trapped in a pit. "I'm certainly not going to follow him!" thought Viraf with a shudder. No sooner were these words formed in his mind than he found himself once again in the company of the old hag, only now they were in Hell. First he experienced intense cold, far worse than he had known in Hamestagan. Next he felt overwhelming heat, like being in a fiery furnace. Then he was plunged into utter darkness so intense that he could almost reach out and grasp it. Into this blackness seeped a foul stench so thick he thought he might choke. From here he was led to the edge of a great pit, which his guide claimed was the greedy jaws of Hell. As he looked down, down to the bottom, he saw thousands of souls all tightly packed in together, moaning and wailing pitifully. "They all believe themselves to be alone down there," cackled the old hag. "After three days of that," she jabbed with a gnarled finger, "they believe they have spent nine thousand years in Hell!" As Viraf continued to watch the wicked souls in torment, presently he became aware of all manner of vile creatures moving among them, some as high as mountains. They tore at the wicked souls, much as the wild beast had on the Chinvat Bridge. Snow and sleet plagued them as well as fires springing up here and there. Stones and ashes fell from all directions, and through it all Viraf could detect the same foul stench.

"What happens to these poor souls?" asked Viraf. "Do they just stay there forever and ever?"

"Oh, no!" wheezed the old hag. "They have to face punishment for their misdeeds."

"What kind of punishment?" Viraf wanted to know.

"It all depends. Look! There! You can see for yourself. There's a woman who committed adultery." Viraf noticed a woman hanging by her breasts while noxious creatures seized her whole body. Next to the woman, he saw a man stretched on a rack while a thousand demons trampled on him with great brutality and violence.

"Why are they doing that?" Viraf wanted to know.

"Because he was selfish with his many riches when he was alive," came the answer.

"What about that man over there? He seems to be measuring nothing but dust and ashes and then stuffing them in his mouth."

"He was a tradesman and he gave false measure, cheating his customers. So now he pays!" The old hag seemed positively delighted with this punishment.

"Look! There's a man in a boiling cauldron. What did he do?"

"He committed adultery, that's what he did."

"But I see one foot is sticking out of the cauldron. Why is that?" "Oh, well, when he was alive, he killed many vile creatures with that foot so it was left outside the boiling cauldron and does not suffer like the rest of his body."

"What about that man being flogged with serpents, what was his offense?"

"Those demons are punishing him for being an unmerciful ruler when he was alive. Nobody escapes his due in this place!" Viraf continued to notice other poor souls being punished in various ways for their misdeeds: a woman for having an abortion, a man for homosexuality, another for meanness. Viraf turned to ask the old hag one more question. She had vanished. In her place stood a fig tree. Viraf blinked, sat up, looked around, and realized he was back in his own garden. The scenes he had so recently experienced, however, were still vividly with him. "I must tell the faithful about what I have witnessed!" thought Viraf. And so Viraf went out of his garden and told the first person he saw of his extraordinary vision. This one told that one, and that one told another, and the story continued to be passed on, and now I have told you.

This tale is based on the teachings of Zoroaster, who lived from c. 628 to c. 551 B.C. Through a series of revelations, he started preaching a religion in which a single Wise Lord, Ahura Mazda, was recognized as the creator of the universe. Pitted against Ahura Mazda was Ahriman and the forces of evil. Many scholars believe that Zoroastrian beliefs greatly influenced both East and West. They suggest that Judeo-Christian descriptions of the afterlife, as well as those found in Hinduism and Buddhism, are based, in part at least, on Viraf's vision of heaven and hell. In Persian Mythology, John Hinnells states, "Life after death has been a dominant part of Persian thought from earliest times. Eternity is not just a promise of a future reward, it is in fact man's true home, for that which appears to destroy man — death — is the weapon of the Evil Spirit. Man was made for life and not for death. If death were the last word then Evil Spirit, not God, would be the ultimate victor."[†]

It is easy to see how both Eastern and Western beliefs about the afterlife could have been influenced by Zoroastrianism, given the geographical location of Persia (modern Iran) between Europe and Asia. It is less clear how other cultures, such as that of the Kogi of South America, come to have similar elements in their soul journey stories. Viraf's description of the River of Tears is very like the Kogi's river of the same name in "Gourd Woman." The details about how to cross the river, fabricated by the author, are different, but the underlying philosophy — excessive or inappropriate mourning deters the soul on its journey — is the same.

[†] Hinnells, John, *Persian Mythology* (London: Hamlyn Publishing Group Ltd., 1973), p. 62.

RECONCILIATION WITH DEATH

For the sword outwears its sheath,
And the heart wears out the breast,
And the soul must pause to breathe,
And love itself have rest.

"So We'll Go No More A-Roving"   LORD BYRON

This section reflects a few of the ways people have coped with their grief in the face of death. "How can I go on living without her?" "It's not fair that I'm left alone!" The excruciating pain of grief is beyond description for those who have experienced it. Starting with Dr. Elisabeth Kubler-Ross and continuing with Stephen Levine, much excellent work has been done in recent years to help people understand and work through the several stages we go through in grieving. Compassionate Friends and other similar groups offer support for those engaged in the grieving process. Perhaps some of these stories and poems may give comfort to those in distress today as they surely did in their original settings.

The Old Woodcutter

Ancient Greek: Aesop

An old man once cut some wood and was walking a long way carrying it. As he grew weary, he put down his load and called Death to come.

When Death appeared and asked why he had called for him, the old man said, "To get you to take up my burden."

From *Aesop Without Morals,* by Lloyd W. Daly (New York: Thomas Yoseoff, 1961). Permission applied for.

This spare fable from Aesop alludes to a common predicament. In the past twenty-five years that I have worked with older people, I have noticed how ready some of them seem to die, even when they are relatively healthy. Their energy goes, they are no longer interested in the activities that formerly they enjoyed, and they don't retain current information, though memories from the distant past may remain vivid. What is it, I used to wonder, that keeps them going? The answer, I realized, could be found often in the attitudes of their children, who refused to acknowledge their parent's decline, so frightened were they by the thought of death. These "children," even though they might have had children and grandchildren of their own, still clung to their elderly parent as a way of feeling safe. I have come to believe such dependency relationships can keep people alive past their time, just as modern artificial life-support systems do, thereby blocking people from making their natural transitions. This dilemma has been with us, it would appear, at least since the days of Aesop. This translation, according to the editor Lloyd Daly, represents a more "authentic" version of the original fable. It is different from other English versions, which suggest a fear of death rather than acceptance.

Side by side they made for the Island of the Blessed.

The Spirit-Bride

Native American: The Algonquins of Ontario

Once there was a young brave named Running Deer, whose bride died on the very day fixed for their wedding. Before this sad event he had been the most courageous and high-spirited of warriors and the most skillful of hunters. But afterward his pride and his bravery seemed to desert him. In vain his friends urged him to seek the chase and begged him to take a greater interest in life. The more they pressed him, the more melancholy he became, till at length he passed most of his time by the grave of his bride.

He was roused from his state of apathy one day, however, by hearing some old men discussing the existence of a path to the Spirit-world, which they supposed lay to the south. A gleam of hope shone in Running Deer's young breast, and worn with sorrow as he was, he armed himself and set off southward. For a long time he saw no appreciable change in his surroundings — rivers, mountains, lakes, and forests similar to those of his own country appeared on all sides. But after a weary journey of many days, he fancied he saw a difference. The sky was more blue, the prairie more fertile, the scenery more gloriously beautiful. From the old men's conversation he had overheard before setting out, Running Deer judged that he was nearing the Spirit-world.

Just as he emerged from a spreading forest he saw before him a little lodge set high on a hill. Thinking its occupant might be able to direct him to his destination,

Adapted from "The Spirit-Bride," in *Myths & Legends of the North American Indians,* by Lewis Spence, pp.162–165 (New York: Thomas Y. Crowell Co., 1914).

he climbed to the lodge and accosted an aged man who stood in the doorway. "Can you tell me the way to the Spirit-world?" inquired Running Deer.

"Yes," answered the old man gravely, throwing aside his cloak of swan's skin. "Only a few days ago she whom you seek rested in my lodge. If you will leave your body here you may follow her." Slowly the old man raised his right arm and pointed. "To reach the Island of the Blessed you must cross yonder gulf you see in the distance. But I warn you the crossing will be no easy matter." The lodge-keeper's eyes seemed to be burning holes into Running Deer's. "Do you still wish to go?"

"Oh, yes, yes," cried the warrior eagerly, and as the words tumbled out of his mouth he felt himself grow suddenly lighter. Then the whole aspect of the scene changed: Everything looked brighter and more ethereal. In no time he found himself walking through thickets, which offered no resistance to his passage. "How strange," thought Running Deer. "This must be what it's like being in the Spirit-world." When he reached the gulf which the old man had indicated, he found, to his delight, a wonderful canoe ready on the shore. Unlike any canoe he had ever seen, it was cut from a single white stone and shone and sparkled in the sun like a jewel. Running Deer jumped into the canoe, and just as he was pushing off from shore he saw his pretty bride enter an exact duplicate of his boat and imitate all his movements. Side by side they made for the Island of the Blessed, a charming woody islet set in the middle of the water, like an emerald in silver.

When they were about halfway across, a sudden storm arose and huge waves threatened to engulf them. Many other people had embarked on the perilous waters by this time, some of whom perished in the furious tempest. But Running Deer and the maiden battled on bravely, never losing sight of each other. Because they were good and innocent, the Master of Life had decreed that they should arrive safely at the fair island, and after a weary struggle they felt their canoes grate on the shore.

Hand in hand the lovers walked among the beautiful sights and sounds that greeted their eyes and ears from every quarter. There was no trace of the recent storm. The sea was as smooth as glass and the sky as clear as crystal. Running Deer and his bride felt that they could wander on in this magical place forever. But at length a faint, sweet voice whispered in Running Deer's ear, "It is time for you to return to Earth-country. You must finish your mortal course. You will become a great chief among your own people. Rule wisely and well, and when your earthly career is over, you shall return to your bride, who will retain her youth and beauty forever."

At first Running Deer felt overwhelmed; he was loathe to leave his newly found love. But he recognized the voice as that of the Master of Life, so sadly he bade farewell to his beloved and set out on his return journey. He was not without hope, however, for he looked forward to another and more lasting reunion.

Returning to the old man's lodge, Running Deer regained his body, went home as the gentle voice on the island had commanded him, and became a father to his people for many years. By his just and kindly rule he won the hearts of all who knew him and ensured for himself a safe passage back to the Island of the Blessed, where he arrived at last to partake of everlasting happiness with his beautiful bride.

In "The Spirit-Bride" we have a Native American version of the descent into the underworld for the sake of the beloved. Stories of this kind include Dante's journeys through Hell, Purgatory, and Paradise under the guidance of Beatrice, and Orpheus's quest for Eurydice. Here, as for Dante and Orpheus, the afterlife is pictured simply as a different physical place — hard to find and difficult to approach but tangible and continuous with the familiar world we see about us. For Running Deer, the journey reconciles him to a long life apart form his bride. He has more trouble accustoming himself to this continued life than he does to the idea of death, since life is to be spent without her. But it is precisely his glimpse of her in the other world, his assurance of perfection that awaits him, that makes him such a practical and involved leader of his people in this world. The story thus refutes those who might imagine that contact with other worlds and beings could alienate us from our earthly responsibilities. On the contrary, it seems to assert that the stronger our sense of continued existence after physical life, the more equipped we will be for the everyday challenges of this world. On two separate occasions I have listened to testimony from two of Dr. John E. Mack's experiencers, people who have been abducted by "alien" beings. Both declared that once they had conquered their initial terror at being exposed to other realities, they heightened their resolve to live more compassionate and responsible lives in this reality. Their expanded consciousness, therefore, seems to have given them both roots and wings. In this way they resemble the Algonquin brave.

Lamentation I

African: The Efik of West Africa

Oh, our dear mother, you have left a big loneliness for us.

Today we have lost one who gives advice from our midst.

Today we have lost our right hand.

What is life good for?

Oh, death, what a loss you have given us.

Why do you have a strong heart against us in this way?

Today you have taken our mother to ghost towns.

Mother, good-bye. Greet relatives in that region for us.

Please our mother, do not forget us.

Remember us as you used to.

Our beloved mother, safe journey.

The good woman whose gait is admired, safe journey.

Our mother with sweet speech, safe journey.

From "Specimens of Efik Folklore" by D. C. Simmons, in *Folk-Lore, A Quarterly Review of Myth, Tradition, Institution & Custom,* vol. 66, 1955 (London: William Glaisher, Ltd.).

In this mourner's lament, we see several of the stages of grief being expressed in rapid succession. At first the attention is on the mourner, who accusingly wails: "You have left a big loneliness for us" and "Today we have lost our right hand." The emphasis here is on the pain of the loss. Then there is a hint of anger mingled with depression with, "What good is life for?" An attempt to negotiate with Death is suggested in "Why do you have a strong heart against us in this way?" At this point the lament shifts and begins to accept the loss with a clear statement of fact. "Today you have taken our mother to ghost towns." From that point the attention moves from self to other, from mourner to deceased, with "Mother, good-bye. Greet relatives in that region for us. Please, our mother, do not forget us. Remember us as you used to." It ends on a note of loving acceptance, "Our mother with sweet speech, safe journey."

Lamentation II

Buddhist: The Tamang of Nepal

Mother, mother, why have you left me? When you were alive,

You lived by your son's word and affection.

Now after death, accept our affectionate offerings.

Don't continue to be attached to your sons and daughters,

Or to your grandsons and daughters,

Or to your various livestock and things!

Don't take rebirth as a mule, or as a dog or as a pig!

Come back again in human life-form!

From *Order In Paradox, Myth, Ritual, and Exchange Among Nepal's Tamang,* by David H. Holmberg, p.207 (Ithaca & London: Cornell University Press, 1989). Used with permission of the publisher, Cornell University Press.

In this lament from Nepal, delivered, we are told, in a stylized chant by women with unbraided hair, there is a different emphasis from the West African lament. Both start out much the same: The mourners feel sorry for themselves. Very quickly, however, the Nepalese version shifts into appreciation for the deceased, then to pleas for the soul to let go of ties to this life in order to take right action culminating in rebirth.

Buddhists believe there is a forty-nine-day period between death and rebirth. The soul has to take this journey alone but can be assisted by certain prayers and ceremonies performed by family and lamas, the spiritual leaders of the community. The Tamang say that the dead person's shadow-soul may not be aware, at first, that it has been separated from its body. The lamas, therefore, recite prayers describing the path to rebirth, call the shadow-soul, and bind it to a new body, in effigy, displaying this new body to the shadow-soul through a mirror. As one lama explained: "They inform the shadow-soul of the different lives it can take. They tell the shadow-soul which are good lives to take and which are bad. It is training after death. Lamas cannot take people to the heavens; they can only tell the way: You are on your own. Don't linger on the way; don't stop halfway. Don't stay with the shades and harmful agents."[†]

[†] Holmberg, David H., *Order in Paradox, Myth, Ritual, and Exchange Among Nepal's Tamang,* (Ithaca, N.Y.: Cornell University Press, 1989), pp. 206–207.

The Other World

Ancient Egyptian

Here are cakes for thy body,
Cool water for thy throat,
Sweet breezes for thy nostrils,
And thou art satisfied.

No longer dost thou stumble
Upon thy chosen path,
From thy mind all evil
And darkness fall away.

Here by the river,
Drink and bathe thy limbs,
Or cast thy net, and surely
It shall be filled with fish.

The holy cow of Hapi
Shall give thee of her milk,
The ale of gods triumphant
Shall be thy daily draught.

From "The Other World," *The Egyptian Book of the Dead,* c. 3300 B.C., translated by Robert Hillyer, as quoted in *The Oxford Book of Death,* chosen and edited by D. J. Enright, pp. 176–177 (Oxford: Oxford University Press, 1983). Permission applied for.

White linen is thy tunic,
Thy sandals shine with gold;
Victorious thy weapons,
That death come not again.

Now upon the whirlwind
Thou followest thy Prince,
Now thou hast refreshment
Under the leafy tree.

Take wings to climb the zenith,
Or sleep in Fields of Peace;
By day the Sun shall keep thee,
By night the rising Star.

The ancient Egyptians believed that the afterlife journey would require the same elements as a journey in this life and so were careful to bury their dead with everything they might need.

This poem is a kind of blessing for the deceased that not only invokes a safe and pleasant setting ("Sweet breezes for thy nostrils") and provides all material comforts ("Here are cakes for thy body and cool water for thy throat") but also calls for spiritual enlightenment ("From thy mind all evil and darkness fall away"). There is a hint of the universal difficulty people have with death in the verse that ends: "Victorious thy weapons, that death come not again."

Let Me Drink Wine

African: Niger Delta

Let me drink wine.

We don't come twice to this world, my brother.

That of today is what I know;

That of tomorrow I cannot know.

He took plantains and went to Igbo-land,

With my ears I heard that Death killed him.

Let me drink wine.

We don't come twice to this world, my brother.

From "Isoko Songs of Ilue-Ologbo," by Philip M. Peek and N.E. Owheibar in *African Arts,* Winter 1971 p. 46, (Los Angeles: University of California). Used with permission.

Here we have the ultimate, pragmatic, rational approach to death. "That of today is what I know; That of tomorrow I cannot know." Even though this lament comes from West Africa, many people in the United States today might agree with its point of view. Often those who are highly trained in the sciences share the belief that nothing happens after death other than the decay of the physical body. It is difficult, however, to find stories that support this viewpoint, though one frequently hears people make remarks such as, "You don't get out of this life alive, you know," or "You're going to be dead a long, long time."

Another curiously modern thought is the line, "With my ears I heard that Death killed him." How often we hear people say, "Cancer took him," or "She had a bad heart." The implication is that the person in question was acted upon by outside forces and not involved in his or her own death. Contrast this point of view with that of the old woodcutter in Aesop's fable (p.127), who by summoning Death, takes an active role in the completion of his time on earth.

It is not clear whether the line, "Let me drink wine," is a call to celebrate the end of an honorable life that is now over, a symbolic act to acknowledge a miserable relationship that at last has been severed, or a despairing gesture to drown the mourner's sorrows with forgetfulness. It could be any or all of these. Who knows what lies deep in the hearts of those gathered for the final rites of the deceased? It is quite possible to have a number of conflicting feelings about someone who has just died. We may feel angry, sad, relieved, and guilty all at the same time. No wonder death takes time for the living to process!

Five Poppy Seeds

Buddhist

Once there was a young woman, the wife of a wealthy man, who became heart-sick because of the death of her child. She took the dead child in her arms and went from house to house begging people to heal the child.

They could do nothing for her, but finally the disciple of a Wise One advised her to see his Master, who was staying nearby. So the woman carried the dead child to the Master.

The Wise One looked upon her with sympathy and said, "To heal the child I need some poppy seeds; go and beg four or five poppy seeds from some home where death has never entered.

So the grief-stricken woman went out and sought a house where death had never entered, but in vain. In home after home, she heard the story of loss and grief. At last she was obliged to return to the sage. In his quiet presence her mind cleared and she understood the meaning of his suggestion. She took the body away and buried it in the earth, then returned to become an ardent seeker after truth.

From *The Teachings of Buddha,* by Buddhist Promoting Foundation, pp. 186–187 (Tokyo: Kosiado Printing Co. 1966).

There are several versions of this tale from various branches of Buddhism. Essentially the message in each is the same. As in so many Buddhist stories, the hard lesson, in this case of facing mortality and overcoming grief, is delivered through the conduit of compassion. Fortunately and unfortunately, the story reminds us, we are never alone in our suffering.

I Dance Despite Death

African: Niger Delta

I dance despite death, mother,

I dance despite death.

On my father's side is death;

On my mother's side is death.

I dance despite death, mother,

I dance despite death.

Whatever happens, I accept it.

From "Isoko Songs of Ilue-Ologbo," by Philip M. Peek and N. E Owheibar in *African Arts,* Winter 1971 (Los Angeles: University of California). Used with permission.

I dance despite death.
Whatever happens, I accept it.